IN PRAISE OF CIVILITY

In Praise of Civility

James W. Heisig

RESOURCE *Publications* • Eugene, Oregon

IN PRAISE OF CIVILITY

Copyright © 2021 James W. Heisig. All rights reserved. Except for brief quotations in critical publications or reviews, no part of this book may be reproduced in any manner without prior written permission from the publisher. Write: Permissions, Wipf and Stock Publishers, 199 W. 8th Ave., Suite 3, Eugene, OR 97401.

Wipf & Stock
An Imprint of Wipf and Stock Publishers
199 W. 8th Ave., Suite 3
Eugene, OR 97401

www.wipfandstock.com

PAPERBACK ISBN: 978-1-6667-3604-5
HARDCOVER ISBN: 978-1-6667-9384-0
EBOOK ISBN 978-1-6667-9385-7

Cover design: Claudio Bado

Contents

- *1* How not to read this book
  - *3* One
  - *21* Two
  - *38* Three
  - *57* Four
  - *75* Five
  - *93* Six
  - *112* Seven
- *129* How to reread this book

How not to read this book

Just to be clear, I did not write this book with an overall framework in mind and was not terribly worried about maintaining any internal logic to keep my thoughts in order. The glue that holds the pages to the spine is as close to a unifying element as any. You should not think that the numbering of the chapters from one to seven represents progress in a straight line. The only purpose was to break it up into bite-size units that could be read in a short sitting. If you insist on looking for a master plan, I leave you to it with only the warning that, having finished, I am not aware of it.

The quotations and stories that garnish this rather disorderly huddle of thoughts are by and large things I have picked up over years, scribbled here and there in the margins of books, or carried into conversations so many times that they no longer can be said to belong to their original source. A final bibliography—let alone, heaven forbid, footnotes—would give altogether the wrong impression of what I know to be an academically promiscuous array of hearsay, actual memories, embellished memories, precise and imprecise citations, twice-told tales, and the like.

I feel I should apologize in advance, but I resist the impulse in the hope that you will find the topic as engaging as I and, now and then along the way, forget that you are reading someone else's words.

James W. Heisig
Nagoya, Japan
1 March 2021

One

After more than five centuries, Erasmus of Rotterdam's *In Praise of Folly* is still a sobering read. Page after page we have to smile and nod our heads, almost in spite of ourselves, as he teases intellectuals for forgetting that for every ounce of reason lodged in the brain there is a pound of passions ranging throughout the whole body. When it comes to being serviceable to the world, he writes, those who fancy themselves erudite run to consult their books and their syllogisms, and while they are still stuck there thinking things over, the fool rushes blindly ahead and does what needs to be done. He reminds us that no matter how much the learned may snicker from the sidelines at the folly of love, they know as well as the rest of us that without that folly society would lose its cement and cohesion. Erasmus takes hold of the high-minded and shakes the moralism out of them, shaming them for forgetting that we human beings are so frail and cross-grained, and so easily wheedled into thinking that we are always right, that not even ordinary friendship is possible without making allowance for one another's faults. He reserves his praise for passion's break with reason to rebel against what is wrong, to enjoy the things of life with the innocence of children, to close an eye to the shortcomings of others.

Stripped of its satire, not to say the irony of so great a scholar lampooning the importance of knowledge, the book's playful tone was not intended to hurt his colleagues and fellow churchmen. The more you read of Erasmus, the easier it is to catch on to his true motives: to nudge his readers into having a good laugh at themselves and trusting more in their better selves.

I would like to take up the praise of civility in that same spirit—though clearly without the rhetorical gifts and wit that Erasmus brought to his writing. To those who identify too closely with their own moral outrage against the evils of society, to the social critics who feel that nothing is truly experienced until it has been turned into a judgment about what is right and what is wrong, civility may look like the sheepish virtue of those too timid to stand up for their rights and for what they believe. Even the calmest and most sanguine of readers may resist the call to civility as the romantic illusion of a fool out of touch with the real world. Later we will have to return to face these misgivings. It just seems to me the wrong place to start.

Admittedly, at first glance an exposé of the nearly epidemic spread of incivility that has come to infect more and more of our citizenry in more and more places might put us on a better footing. For one thing, incivility is a far side easier to spot than civility is. When Tolkien paused in the middle of *The Hobbit* to reflect on how his tale was getting along, he shone a light on our dark disposition to fix attention on certain things in life and skip lightly over others:

> Now it is a strange thing, but things that are good to have and days that are good to spend are soon told about, and not much to listen to; while things that are uncomfortable, palpitating, and even gruesome, may make a good tale, and take a deal of telling anyway.

Bad behavior is always easier to diagnose than good. It certainly makes for more engaging conversation. When it comes to praising the virtue of others, we have a rather limited vocabulary compared to the rich thesaurus within our reach to censure their wrongdoings. The principles governing good conduct are more transparent where they are offended and tend to fog up where they are honored. In any case, the simplest and most straightforward way to introduce civility would seem to be by defining it as the absence of incivility, and the surest way to commend it, by giving its opposite a good scolding.

This was Erasmus' strategy but will not be ours. He delivered his praise of folly by keelhauling rationality up and down the shoreline in order to enhance the use of reason, not replace it with unreason. I have no intention of trying to restore incivility to its proper place by exposing the limits of civility. Like any attempt to understand "right" action as "wrong" action with the lining turned out, pursuing civility through its absence ends up surrendering to the pessimistic belief that doing what is right begins by resisting the temptation to do what is wrong.

Put the other way around, unless we can find our way back to a primal instinct for harmony with our surroundings, any praise we have to offer is doomed from the start.

In a word, the pursuit of civility needs to pay closer attention to its actual practice rather than to its neglect. And that is all I want to do in these pages: to tell stories about civility that provoke second thoughts about the effects of incivility on our lives and the lives of those around us. But before we start asking how to recognize incivility and confront it, we need to have some idea of how to ask the question in a civil manner. Confronting one incivility with another is like trying to cure a disease by spreading it. Praising a virtue by condemning its neglect is pointless unless we can first describe it on its own terms.

We are seriously mistaken if we look on civil as a private virtue that does little to help us take charge of the things of life. As short quips of moral outrage overtake more and more of our "civilized" conversation, the slow plod of thinking and acting civilly is easily left behind like a quaint and simpleminded distraction from the business of standing up for ourselves. This is precisely the prejudice I wish to turn on its head, and I cannot think of any better way to do it than to gather examples of civility in action.

At one time or another, I have been guilty of many of the incivilities criticized in these pages. So, when I say "we," it is not a polite way of pointing a finger at the reader. I am being serious. Of course, the mix of humanity and inhumanity is different for each of us, but the basic ingredients are pretty much the same for the saint and the sinner, the sage and the fool. What is more, none of us is without the darkness of deeds thrown into shadow by the shining beliefs and ideals we profess to others.

The conventional wisdom is that one should not inflict principles on others that one does not practice oneself. The famous first-century scholar and miracle-worker Rabbi Hanina Ben-Dosa put it this way:

> When a person's deeds exceed their wisdom, their wisdom will endure; but when a person's wisdom exceeds their deeds, that wisdom will not stand.

This seems all wrong to me. Our ideals are *always* higher than our attempts to realize them. Even at our best, we only skid on the thin edge of our ideals. If I did not believe that, if I felt I had to rid myself of all hypocrisy before talking about my ideals, I would take my hands off the keyboard right now and lay them over my mouth. If we take the adage "Practice before you preach" at face value, our only choice would be to make light of the little wisdom we have or at least keep it to ourselves. Better that we breathe in our ideals and breathe them out again in practice as best we can, like an accordion that fills up soundlessly with air and only makes music when the airway is opened to the outside. The melodies we produce are never a match for the best we can imagine, but that is a poor excuse for not giving voice to our ideals. The only wisdom that endures, *pace* the holy rabbi, is a wisdom that is not silenced by its failure in practice. My words are always so much better than I am, but I cannot discount this as a mere failure on my part. It is a part of life, one of the roles we play (which is what the word *hypocrisy* meant in Greek) and not a poison that infects the whole stew of roles that make up our lives.

This may have something to do with why we prefer stories with endings. We know very well that the ending is not a real ending, that even death catches us with one foot in the air, about to take the next step. But we like to believe in endings because we cannot bring ourselves to admit that we *never* get close to living out our own ideals, let alone those we were taught from the time we were children. There is hypocrisy built into our very nature simply because we *want* things to end perfectly, but we *know* they will not. This should humble us, but instead the desire for an ending is inflicted on those around us who fail to live up to what is expected of them. Rather than monitor the road to a proper ending of events, civility asks us to close the circle on what is right in front of us, to find a way for the moment to bring harmony.

Which of us would not be embarrassed by the raw truth of the disconnect between our words and our deeds? But does that mean we stop seeking the truth and sharing what we find until we have lived up to it?

The civility I wish to praise here is a far cry from moral heroism or angelic virtue. On the contrary, it is a matter of ordinary, everyday decency that is well within reach. Without it, even the noblest of heroic action quickly collapses into self-righteousness. As arguments go, the appeal to anecdotes may seem a bit scrappy. But then again, our aim is not to lay out a clear set of rational principles for behavior that can be defended in the abstract and then applied with some level of confidence to our concrete interactions with others. It is rather to find our way to acting fluently with our surroundings, like one string vibrating effortlessly to the hum of another. The habit of civility is the behavioral equivalent of what William James called the "sentiment of rationality," the labor-saving device that allows us to find a balance between the need for simple and manageable ideas on the one hand, and a clear picture of reality in its fullness, on the other. It is not a renunciation of reason but a practical use of reason achieved by infusing the irrational—the "passion" of which Erasmus spoke—into the rational.

I do not mean to imply that having the conviction of one's beliefs is the natural enemy of civility. But certitude *is*. Nothing blinds us to our "frail and cross-grained" nature like the principled refusal to accept the limitations of our ability to understand the things of life. To enshrine our struggles against injustice and morality in certitude at some point or other ends up poisoning civility. In the name of some higher truth to which we are convinced beyond all doubt we have access, we dissolve our aboriginal instincts to live in harmony with others into our lower instincts to impose on others conformity to our own modes of thought and behavior. I am not speaking only of nationalist or imperialist ideologies. Even a religion that spreads a message of universal love can be corrupted by its dream of a perfect catechism into fanatical intolerance against those with dissenting beliefs. Civility is not a cause but an essential quality for protecting all the causes that flow in and out of history from one age to the next against their dark side. Even when it is orphaned by the pressing moral concerns of the day, civility remains right there in front of us, in examples of everyday life that are ours for the emulating. If I did not have the conviction of that belief, I would have thrown up my arms in despair long ago at the collective future of our human race.

You may not agree with me that our collective experiment with human existence is well served by the deliberate renunciation of certitudes regarding the uncertainties of life. You may argue that such renunciation is not possible—or even desirable—on a large scale. I ask only that you indulge me a while longer, until we get into the heart of the matter where these airy discussions of truth and certitude will find a more suitable environment than I have given them so far. Even so, you may end up unpersuaded. I have spent my life juggling a great variety of ideas and perspectives. Perhaps it is a matter of temperament, but I have found it more satisfying to hold a number of possibilities in mind at the same time than to try my hand at constructing a uniform edifice for others to walk around in and form their own opinion of the design. This little book and its defense of the ordinary sense of civility is one example of that. However forceful my manner of expression, I warn you not to expect more than a juggle.

Be that as it may, before we start listing all the things civility *can't* accomplish, we should take seriously what it *can*. And it's a lot more than many of us are used to giving it credit for.

A few years ago I was standing in one of the lines off to the side of an elevator in a department store in Japan, waiting for the carriage to reach our floor. Just then a young woman pushing a baby in a stroller walked by in a short tank top and ripped jeans. Her hair was spiked bright red and blue. She had on black lipstick and wore a ring through her lower lip. Absorbed in whatever was playing on her earphones, she seemed oblivious to the world around her as she strutted up and stopped right in front of the elevator doors. An elderly woman waiting on a bench along the wall behind us put down her newspaper and laid into her.

"Just what do you think you are doing? Have you no manners?"

Everyone lowered their heads stunned, shifting their eyes stealthily back and forth between the baby carriage and the bench, careful to avoid looking at either of the parties directly but anxious to see what would happen next. The old woman raised her voice and carried on.

"Honestly, young people today. So selfish. They don't think of anyone but themselves. Can't you see that you are blocking the doors by stepping right in front of all these people, without so much as a beg-your-pardon?"

No one said a word, but I could sense a bond of confused sympathy among the onlookers. Of course, the old woman was right. And yet it is only common courtesy to step aside for a mother with a baby....

And what do you suppose the young woman said in reply to the tongue-lashing she had just been given in public? Not what you might expect.

She took out her earphones, lowered her eyes, and bowed to the old woman. "My apologies. I'm sorry." As she retreated to the back of the line, she turned to those standing to the right of the doors and repeated the apology, and then again to those in line at the left.

Everyone nodded lightly to acknowledge her. The old woman smiled at the offender, bent her head and shoulders lightly as if to issue an apology to everyone present, and then picked up her newspaper and went on reading.

That is what I mean by civility.

I was not being sarcastic when I suggested that the way the situation resolved itself was not what you might expect. I only meant that there were any number of ways the scene could have played out. Onlookers could have gotten involved to support the mother and baby or to side with the old woman. The young woman herself could have snapped back in self-defense or simply turned her back on the recriminations being hurled in her direction. Put yourself in her position and imagine what you would feel at being embarrassed that way in the presence of total strangers, and how you would expect yourself to react had you been the mother with the stroller. And now pull back and ask yourself if her withdrawal and inaction was not precisely what was best for everyone involved, including herself. Had one of the others immediately stepped aside and invited the mother to take their place in line, this would have shamed the old woman. If some of the bystanders had scowled at her, it would have provoked others to make their own judgment on the matter. Instead, the whole situation and everyone in it was swept up in something larger than the conflict at hand. Sure, the old lady wanted to teach the young mother a lesson, as people seem to do more and more the older they get. In fact, it was the young mother who taught her, along with the rest of us, without even realizing it. In accepting responsibility in full, along with the small flush of embarrassment it brought her, she allowed calm to be restored.

To me, her response remains in memory as an example of basic human goodness—something worthy of emulation because it was so very ordinary and spontaneous, and yet so unexpectedly reassuring of the power of simple civility.

To know civility, it is not as important to delve into motivations or examine the consistency between principles and action as it is to look at the receipts. You know civility when you see it. It is one of those things you feel in your bones before you can analyze it or put it into words. In fact you cannot really understand it without getting back to the point where you can say that something *felt* right before you decided to stop and judge whether it *was* right and to explain *why*.

Civility is a kind of moral art. It is not the sort of behavior that can be clearly defined and then pursued or taught on the basis of that definition and its corollary practices. Not that it's undefinable, but any definition we come up with tells us very little of what we need to know.

Think of the dictionary definition of the word *grandmother*: "the mother of one of your parents." In the abstract, yes, but that's chalk-and-cheese different from what the word actually means. In pretending to cover everything, it says too little. For me, *grandmother* means an apple pie cooling on the ledge by the window, a heap of leaves under a large oak tree in the back garden where I could jump in and frolic around, a trip to the store to get something my mother wouldn't buy for me, the awkwardness of being hugged against a large bosom, a picture of Liberace sitting on the dining room buffet, a case of old knickknacks and souvenirs in the living room next to a television playing a soap opera, a saggy old mattress with motley colored blankets, and—well you get the point. And that is only one of my grandmothers and only the meaning it had for me as a young boy. Not to mention the memories *you* associate with the word. A grandmother is a whole constellation of impressions, recollections, and images that you can walk around in without ever being able to put it all into words—or ever really seeing the need to.

Civility is like that. We know it when we see it and we know more about it each time we see it. What we do about what we see is, of course, important, but so is just *seeing it*.

It should be obvious that the young mother's mistake was more than just a lapse in manners. It was as thoughtless as the old woman's lambaste was nasty. By the same token, the way they resolved the situation was more than just polite but also less than gallant. It was civil, nothing more, nothing less. Politeness, manners, and gallantry neutralize incivility each in its own way. But what we saw that day in the department store was not courtesy, good breeding, or heroism. On the contrary, it was so unremarkably natural and so obviously within reach of all of us, that anyone who was witness to must have known instinctively that she had done the right thing. I remember, for a fleeting moment, thinking better of myself, almost as if out of nowhere a cool breeze had passed over me on a hot on a summer's day. I am used to thinking better of myself when my judgments or my deeds have triumphed over some adversity or ignorance large or small. But that day, for reasons I still cannot quite explain, I felt proud of just being human and of having to wipe my eyes as I boarded the elevator.

There are times, of course, when we see civility in action and don't like what we see. Granted the young mother in our example did the right thing. But in other circumstances, especially those that involve us personally and challenge our sturdiest convictions of what is right or rational, our minds instinctively rebel against the idea of being good and reasonable by not taking action or withholding judgment. The step is such a short one: Yes, but what if the mother had been from another country and was not aware of local customs? What if the old woman were someone who sat there for hours just waiting for someone to offend the "rules"? What if she did not have a baby in the stroller but a large bag of groceries? What if...? This is how we protect ourselves against assaults on the self-righteousness of our everyday habits of thought. We withdraw from what has taken place right before our eyes into a cloud of abstraction and create scenarios of our own that allow us to carry on as before, unrepentant, impenetrable, almost as if our habits of thought were a semi-permeable membrane that allow us free access to the world around but does not allow the outside to come in.

We all know what it is to resist the claims that encounters with genuine goodness put on us. We find it easier to beat a retreat into the world of categorical or generic thinking, where the imagination quickly chokes the life out of what we feel by shifting our attention to a hypothetical "But what if...?" Faced with even minor irritations, how often do we not choose to plant our feet firmly and stand on principle rather than take a step back and muffle our impulse to join in and take sides. Much as we hate to admit it, our interference often has less to do with endorsing right over wrong and truth over falsehood than with the simple urge to inject ourselves into situations that would likely straighten themselves quicker without us. The high-minded generalizations we carry around with us for guidance end up spreading an infection that a modicum of civility might otherwise have helped soothe. And all the while, in our heart, we knew better.

Heraclitus had it right twenty-five hundred years ago: "Everything flows." That is the way it is with the things of life. Whatever they are, whatever else you may think of them, one thing is clear: they are constantly on the move. That is what things do and there is really nothing we can do to stop it. We cannot even define them adequately in their native surroundings any more than we can write their names on the surface of a river. It is at once the curse and the blessing of mind that we are able to draw things out of the stream, set them on the ground, and dry them off for a closer look before tossing them back in. This allows us, we tell ourselves, to look at particular things "in the concrete," when in fact this drawing out is how we think of things "in the abstract": it is our way of looking away from the concrete—the whole muddled and tangled concrescence they belong to—in order to manage them for our own purposes. Without this gift, we would not be able to talk or make tools or even dream.

At the same time, the more deeply rooted our habits of categorical thinking, the less prepared we are for novelty. In searching for the words to describe events, we grasp for definitions, with the result that before we know it, whatever novelty there was to be discovered gets vaporized and floats effortlessly into the ideas and values we had before anything had happened. This is what makes the genuine experience of novelty so powerful: it tosses us back into the river. For what may only be a fleeting moment, mind is part of the "everything flows." It is only when we are safely back at home on dry land that we can breathe easily and recover our language to talk about what just happened. Novelty is always a kind of foreign country. It makes us realize how much the habits of daily culture control our thoughts and our actions. The abstractions and definitions on which generic thinking relies become transparent to us when they do not work as we expect them to.

The raw goodness I felt in the brief exchange between the old woman and the young mother was just such an experience of novelty. What made the goodness *raw* was that it didn't really belong to anyone in particular but to an event that crystallized before our eyes. It was not a matter of apportioning blame or taking credit. We just stood and watched goodness happen, as much a part of it as the two protagonists. For my part, I remember only being caught off guard, speechless and without a word or thought to hold on to. It all took place in less than a minute, but as I think back on it now, I cannot help thinking how much more in character it would have been for me to have escaped into the airy castles of categorical judgments, there to sort out right from wrong, and then to walk away unaffected, with only a curio of a memory to take with me. If things had not gone as they did, if incivility had taken over for one reason or another, I would have been spared the shock of novelty and surely done just that.

Oddly enough, it would have been more comfortable, or at least more predictable, if one of the parties had *not* backed down and accepted responsibility, or if others had stepped in with their own opinion. But the momentary self-satisfaction one might get from hushing the old lady or joining her to badger the young mother would have been no good for anyone. What is it that would make me think for a moment that turning the conflict into a litigation would be "good" for me or for society at large? Why exaggerate the importance of the problem by making it about principles of proper behavior, when a word and a bow were enough to tranquilize the hurt feelings and leave both sides chastised without anyone else having had to weigh in?

Abstracting, literally, is our way of pulling ourselves out of the concrete. I am amazed how often I go out to eat with friends or colleagues and the conversation turns from what we are eating to what we ate last week or what we would like to eat next. Once the food has been tasted and sufficiently remarked on, someone will talk about another restaurant, and someone else another, until the food right in front of us becomes invisible and unsurprising. I remember driving with some friends through the Swiss Alps one winter and stopping the car to get out and admire the majesty of an immense valley spread out before us and blanketed in a fresh coat of snow broken only by a scattering of houses with smoke rising from their chimneys. Sure enough, it wasn't long before someone broke the silence. "Imagine how spectacular this must look in the spring with the hills covered in flowers!" Why is it that we prefer being reassured that we are in control to simply being moved? Is it not the same impulse that authorizes us to exorcise the smallest offenses through the invocation of moral principle that also drives us to imagine ourselves right out of the concrete and into the arms of some abstraction or other?

At bottom, this is the same impulse that drives science forward. It is only by interrupting the concrescence, freezing the flow, breaking it down, and converting it into discreet bits of data that we are able to formulate the underlying laws and principles that allow us to gain some measure of control over the haphazard flux of the world about us. Science is not advanced by anecdotes. If anything, they block the way to objective experimentation and prediction.

In contrast, human wisdom—and nowhere more than when it is lived out—does not advance by the accumulation of data or the discovery of laws based on what we have managed to collect and sort. It is advanced by anecdote, and nowhere more than in those situations so dense that the essence of our humanity seems to be squeezed into the telling. Like the young woman with the spiked hair and ripped jeans bowing her head to something that mattered more than she.

Two

Many years ago, while in London to take a break from my studies, I happened to be walking towards Trafalgar Square and paused at a narrow side street to let a taxi pass. And then another and another. As I was waiting for a break in the traffic to dash across, I noticed an elderly woman standing to my side. Like me, she would only get as far as putting one foot into the road before having to draw it back to avoid being struck. She was short and bent over, and obviously too frail to make a run for it. I took her gently by the arm and with my other hand signaled the approaching vehicle to slow down and let us pass. We made our way slowly and, in a few seconds, had reached the other side. Before I could let go of her arm and wish her good afternoon, she abruptly jerked herself away from me and hobbled off up the street. Why, the old witch! I thought to myself. It's as if I had dragged her against her will. Not even so much as a thank-you....

But I learned something that day, and it is *I* who have to thank *her* for it. I was steaming as I walked across the square to the National Gallery where a friend was waiting for me, mumbling to myself about the ingratitude I had suffered. Perhaps it was the soft spray from the fountain the wind blew over me, but as abruptly as she had pulled her arm away from mine, I suddenly felt drawn away from my annoyance.

I sat down on the edge of the water near one of the bronze lions to cool off. Why did I help her, I asked myself. If it was because she needed help, then as long as she accepted the help, what difference does it make if she thanked me or not? If she *had* thanked me, I would never have thought to ask such a question. I would have strutted off proudly in the shining armor of self-satisfaction, not realizing that the assistance I have given the old woman was receipt enough. Everything else was ego and threatened to overtake what was really no more than an ordinary, spontaneous act of civility.

Civility often offers us just such a chance to get over ourselves. It is not so much something *we do*, but something that *happens* when we get over ourselves and get out of the way. In this sense, it is different from being thoughtful towards someone we are in a human relationship with, even if that relationship only begins when you are standing together at the curb trying to dodge the taxis. Being thoughtful is more deliberate, more conscious, and as such enhances our moral character and affects the quality of a relationship. Civility is simpler, less demanding of reflection. It isn't rational or irrational, thoughtful or thoughtless. It is not about ethics or virtue or strengthening bonds. It is about dusting ego off the things we do, without even giving a second thought to the purity of our motivations. That is its special virtue. There are two ways to wash dishes. You can wash them in order to do something good for someone else; or you wash them in order to get them washed. The one says, I washed the plates; the other, the plates are washed. To say something is simpler does not mean that it is easier. Picking up a refrigerator is simple, but hard; tying your shoelaces is complicated, but easy, especially if you don't stop to think of what you are doing. In the case of civility, acting spontaneously is the easy part. Observing the receipts without second thoughts about your own role is a lot harder.

The admonition to get over yourself we are talking about here is not a demanding, lifelong struggle that calls for great discipline and inner spiritual strength. Most confrontations in our daily lives—from a mere jostle over words to the clash of opposing opinions to the frustration at another's actions—are really far more banal and unimportant than we may think at the moment. Compared to those minor irritations where good manners are put to the test, or to those weightier situations where we are locked in debate over some cause we are passionate about, situations that call for civility are much more commonplace. It is when we infect the banal and the unimportant with ego that they flame up into a great conflagration, which we then need to step in and smother. We may find ourselves annoyed when someone goes to pieces at the slightest provocation and wish they would just "get over it." But how rarely we get annoyed at ourselves for turning a trivial slight into a battle cry to stand our ground on principle.

As arguments go, this way of pleading the cause of civility may all seem too obvious, and probably also too naive. From the time we were children, people have been telling us we should just be nicer and kinder to one another. Then we came to face the *real* world where we learned how weak that advice made us look and how meager the rewards for taking it. So, with a nod to our upbringing, we refine our manners, but only so far as they leave ample room for sarcasm and irony to do the work of a head-on collision without having to answer for the consequences. And where that is not enough, we can just set kindness aside altogether.

To be clear, civility is not a childhood fantasy. Like kindness, its elder sister, it is not always polite or pleasant. It is obliged, at times, to teach, and its lessons can fall hard on the unprepared. All I want to insist on here is that civility flourishes on the largest scale when it is allowed to take place without any conceit on the part of those who bring it to bear on the unpleasantries of life. An example comes to mind of how selfless kindness lays bare the foundations of civility.

It happened one summer during an extended stay on the Island of Crete, where I had retreated to complete a long essay on the poet Nikos Kazantzakis for a Greek literary journal. His widow Eleni, who was living in exile at the time in Geneva, had arranged for me to take lodgings in a small house on Heraklion's northern shore. One day I took a bus down to the ruins of the Palace of Knossos. An archaeologist at my college in Cambridge had introduced me to the romantic accounts of Heinrich Schliemann and the more exacting research of Arthur Evans. I was anxious to see for myself what was left of the great labyrinth that had held the fabled Minotaur and inspired Kazantzakis' account of the "bull rite" in his sprawling, epic poem, *The Odyssey: A Modern Sequel*. I sat down under the carving of the bull and the tree of life and wrote in my diary while three groups of French tourists walked among the rubble snapping pictures, paying as little attention as possible to the long-winded historical explanations of their guide.

Before I knew it, the sun had sunk low in the sky and there was a chill in the air. I could hear the sluggish chug of a motor in the distance and made a rush for the bus stop. I was too late—and it was the last bus of the day. So there I stood in my t-shirt, starting to shiver and wondering where to go for help. As it grew darker, I hoped a light from a nearby house would show itself, but all I could see was the eerie outline of the olive trees, their shadows moving with the setting sun like humpback witches roaming the hills. The only sound, the clang of a goat's bell off in the distance. It was more than five kilometers back to Heraklion, but I had no way of knowing where the stony, unlit road made its turn to the city. I sat down under a tree, trying to gather my wits and daring for the walk through the darkness ahead.

Just then I hear a sound coming from the south. The closer it approached, I could make out what seemed to be a cart being pulled by a donkey with a rough and unassuming peasant in the driver's seat. When he caught sight of me, he shouted something to the donkey and drew the cart to a halt. He asked where I was going and when I answered "Heraklion," he let out a deep belly laugh. "Missed the last bus, eh...? All right, hop in."

I climbed up eagerly and squatted down, holding on to the side boards to keep my balance as the cart careened gently to and fro over the rocky route back to the world of heat and light and human company. The floor smelled a mixture of fodder and manure, but I breathed it in without a care, comfortable in the knowledge that I had been spared having to trust my hopeless sense of direction through the black of night. After a half hour or so, I called out to the driver.

"When we get to Heraklion, I know a nice little bar near the Bethlehem Gate. I hope you will let me invite you to a carafe or two of ouzo."

The driver turned his head half-way around and grumbled, "Keep your eye on the wheel."

I looked down at the wooden wheel on one side and then on the other. They seemed sturdy enough and firmly fixed to the axle. Still, I kept an eye on them as I had been told. After some time had passed, I tried again to engage the driver.

"You know what? I would like nothing better than a good *andikristo* of roast goat and mutton. I know a place..."

This time he turned his rough-hewn, swarthy face full around and bellowed at me, "Just keep your eye on the wheel."

I was quiet the rest of the way. When we arrived at the Venetian Walls that surround the city, I jumped out and started to extend my invitation a third time.

"I really don't know how to thank you, but if you would let me...."

He smiled down at me and let out another belly laugh.

"Look at you, a poor student, I should guess, struggling to get by. And you want to buy *me* supper! Hah! Weren't you listening to me when I told you to keep your eye on the wheel? Someday you will have your own donkey cart and come upon a hapless young fellow shivering in the dark of night, and you will give him a ride to wherever he needs to go. Keep your eye on the wheel. It will take a turn and on that day you will thank me. Not before. *Antío!*"

And with that he turned his cart back around and disappeared down the road we had just traveled.

I stood there for a moment, stunned and breathless. I took out my notebook and wrote: *Today I met a farmer driving a donkey cart. He changed my life.*

The farmer's act of selfless kindness gets to the heart of civility by illustrating what a difference getting over oneself makes. The way he helped me on the road to Heraklion and the way I had helped the old lady across the street are poles apart. He erased the need for gratitude by ignoring the goodness of what he had done for me. It was like a swipe at the back of my head. I was the one in trouble, not only because I was stuck out in the cold in the dark of night, but also because I was too full of myself to accept his help without insisting again and again that I repay him.

In my defense, I had been brought up to express gratitude as a way of acknowledging the receipt of a favor shown to me. I knew from long experience what courtesy could do. His refusal of that common courtesy taught me something it could *not* do. It wasn't something I learned from his discourtesy, the way I had with the old lady I helped across the street in London. But neither was it like the wisdom I had picked up as a child swinging on the front porch in my grandfather's lap. In this case, there was no teacher. Or rather, it was the whole setting that did the teaching. The farmer holding the reins on the donkey cart was so far over himself that he was able to grasp effortlessly the whole of what was going on and talk about it without a hint of conceit. The reason his words changed my life was that he had no desire to make them *his* words. As far as he was concerned, they just happened to be passing through him on their way to me. Only later did it become clear that, in the most literal sense of the words, there had been no one to thank. The only possible gratitude one could show such a selfless act would have to be directed at whatever it is in our nature that lets us know true kindness when we see it. This is what I have been calling civility, and it should be obvious that it is worlds away from the politeness and manners of civilized citizenry that the word's etymology suggests. It wasn't important that *he taught me*, but only that *I was taught*, and for that to happen he had to remove himself, naturally, from the lesson.

A decade later I was settled in my academic position at a research institute and living in a home with room to spare for visitors. In no time at all, the wheel turned and I had my eye on it. First, there was a young woman was in trouble and feared for her life. Then a student who was caught penniless and waiting for his family to bail him out. Then an older couple, a string of foreign students, another woman fleeing an abusive family, and... Well, for the next two years or so I was reminded again and again of the road to Heraklion. Each time, my parting words to the visitors were the same words the farmer had spoken to me. "Keep your eye on the wheel." I never thought of it before, but as I write these lines it strikes me that not one of them ever wrote back to thank me. I suppose they all found their own way of answering to the turn of the wheel. Just the thought makes me smile.

Lacking a foundation in selfless kindness, civility can never amount to more than good manners and common courtesy. There is nothing particularly selfless or kind about waiting until everyone gets to the table before you start eating, or about using the silverware rather than stuffing the mashed potatoes into your mouth with both hands. Nor, you may object, does selfless kindness need to come into play when you have to decide how to react to rudeness or boorishness. It's not just that some people are born without manners—we all are. But whoever the cause or whatever the offense, there are always going to be incivilities in your life that threaten your sense of civility on the surface or down to its very marrow. You can be ostensibly civil to those with bad manners and all the while your impeccable manners can be fundamentally uncivil. True, when there is nothing more at stake than a breach of convention, it is easy to put on a display of civility. But this does not mean that it is only in the face of serious conflict or genuine evil that the selfless mettle of true civility is put to the test. That was the point of the two examples above, neither of which posed any threat to society at large, but both of which laid bare the core of civility in the most unspectacular of circumstances better than any encounter with crass or discourteous behavior could.

We all know stories of people having to make split-second decisions where their survival depends on the right choice. You may even have a story of your own to tell. But we get everything backwards when we allow such examples to pattern our reaction to any of the multitude of minor frustrations, inconveniences, little affronts, and clashes of opinion that confront us from day to day. The expectation that your survival instinct, your commitment to principles, and a modicum of good manners are sufficient to see you through already disposes you towards generic thinking, which in turn disposes you against the *collective thinking* from which civility flowers.

I beg you to suspend the connotations you ordinarily attach to the word "collective," which probably suggest some sort of herd mentality. If you dig into the origins of the word, you may recognize the Latin compound for "binding together." Unlike generic thinking, whose clarity comes from focusing on a point of conflict or specific agent, and then rising above the particularity of the situation to a more comprehensive perspective, collective thinking struggles to stay right where it is, to gather up the relevant particulars in the freshness of what it is that binds them together just here and nowhere else. It plants the mind not high up a tower of unchanging principles but low on the ground, in the very "place" where things are taking place. All of this happens in the blink of an eye. We begin thinking one way or the other before we even know what we are doing. All the more reason to take a step back now and again to reconsider the importance of collecting before we act.

When I was a boy, I was fond of stories of Francis of Assisi, that extraordinary thirteenth-century holy man who talked to the sun and the moon—and to animals! I remember trying to talk to pets myself, only to realize that I lacked the requisite sainthood to get through to them. As I grew older, I came to understand that the better skill was his ability to *listen* to them. Where was he standing to do that? Could I find that place? One particular legend of the many that have come down to us suggests an answer.

As the story goes, the Umbrian town of Gubbio was being terrorized by a wolf. It would steal into the town at night and drag away the livestock, sometimes even one of the villagers. People were afraid to leave their homes after sunset. In desperation they went to Francis for help. That very night at dusk he walked out into the hills in search of the wolf. A small band of villagers followed behind at a safe distance. He came to the mouth of a hollow in the hillside and knelt down. Soon the wolf emerged and stood facing him. Francis made the sign of the cross and looked into the eyes of the wolf. After a short while he stretched out his hand to receive the paw of the tranquil beast. Then Francis turned to the townsfolk and explained that the wolf was hungry, and that if they would only leave food for him each night at the foot of the hills, he would leave them in peace. And so they did, and the wolf became part of Gubbio.

Over the centuries, the story was embellished into a miracle story until we no longer know what facts, if any, lay behind it. That doesn't mean the truth behind it has diminished with time: finding the place where you can see things collectively involves knowing how to listen and what to listen to. Had Francis listened only to the people, he would only have known about *their* problem, which was to get rid of the wolf. But he collected the wolf's problem and made it part of their own, and with that everything changed.

Francis began with the sign of the cross. Popular piety sees this as the invocation of a divine power, but I think it is much more down to earth. Marking his forehead and breast and shoulders in the form of a cross had the effect of emptying his mind, much the same way a Zen monk does before wrestling with a *kōan* riddle. It is a symbolic gesture of the will to get over oneself: "I–empty–myself–of myself." Everything remains in place. Nothing is added and nothing is taken away. But the mental bonds that held the parts together are loosened so that everything can be recollected and reconsidered. A hollow opened up within Francis for the voice of the wolf to echo in.

The allusion to a saint is not meant to imply that there is anything morally colossal about getting over yourself in order to shift from generic thinking to a kind of collective thinking. I continue to insist that it is within reach of the commonplace virtue that most of us bring to the conflicts that life throws our way. Still, without the occasional deliberate effort to overcome yourself, there is little chance of forming the kinds of habits that allow you to respond naturally, in the blink of an eye, with genuine civility. There might not be any wild animals terrorizing your neighborhood, but equivalents surround us on all sides on a daily basis. I recall a Buddhist story that crystallizes the practicality of finding a place to stand and listen before speaking and acting.

A man and wife were having trouble communicating. Their verbal spats became more and more frequent and were ending less and less amiably. Finally, the man had had enough and went to visit a hermit living in the forest for help. The holy man listened patiently before offering his advice.

"I want you to go home, and for thirty days *listen* to what your wife is saying. Do not reply. Try to not even react in your own mind. Just listen. Then come back and tell me what you have learned."

The man left despondent. Such unremarkable counsel from someone reputed to be a sage! The confrontations with his wife intensified until at last he agreed to take the advice and hold his tongue. Within a few days, he was able to quell his impulse to carry on the debate silently in his own mind. When the month had passed, he returned to the forest and sought out the hermit.

"You were right. I had really no idea what she was trying to say. I was talking over her even when I wasn't actually interrupting her. Things are so much better now. I am deeply grateful."

With that he turned to leave when the monk stopped him.

"Wait, you have only finished half your work. Now I want you to return home and, for the next thirty days, listen to all the things your wife does *not* say."

No matter whom we are speaking with, there is always something going on between the lines. For whatever reason, we may be content to leave it there and not bring it to the surface. But often even when we want to, when we most desperately want to, we cannot. You inflect your voice, you gesture, but part of what you are trying to say always seems to slip away unsaid. This can gnaw at your self-esteem and damage your relationships with those who seem incapable of listening to what you are not saying. You cannot control the attentiveness of others, but you can see to your own, which, without your having to say a word, can serve others as a mirror, which reflects all the brighter for your ability to get *over* yourself and *under*stand what is going on around you. The more you get over yourself and learn to listen, the more you are able to recollect what is going on around you without having to classify it first, the more you will free others to read between the lines of what you yourself are trying to say.

By now you may be wondering what to do with all this generic praise for non-generic thinking, squeezed out of a few far-fetched anecdotes. I admit, my reasoning so far had provided little solid ground for a general theory about the nature of civility and its connection to moral principles, good manners, selfless kindness, collective thinking, and now attentiveness. Even the most archetypal examples are no substitute for rational argument. Then again, rational argument is no substitute for knowing civility when you see it.

For my part, I am of one mind with Erasmus that folly is not something to be studied but something to be savored. So, too, civility. The young mother in the spiked hair and ripped jeans, the swarthy peasant with his donkey cart, Saint Francis staring into the eyes of the wolf, the husband straining to listen to his wife's silence—each of these images rises just far enough above the particulars of time and place to leave us room to substitute particulars from our own accumulated experience. We react to them with a natural sympathy because we already know what they are talking about. It's just that we don't know how they fit with the very real demands of ordinary life. They draw us into the magic of "Once upon a time," putting us in touch with something that always happens even though it never happened to us or perhaps never even happened at all.

Thinking in anecdotes is different from thinking in proverbs. For one thing, anecdotes require imagination; we have to enter into them to understand them. The truths passed down in proverbs, or bits of wisdom that we absorb as if they were proverbs, are more in the nature of cookie cutters that can be pressed onto any surface once the details have been lumped together and flattened out. We get precisely what we expect from them, no more, no less. Whether we cite a proverb to support our current course of action or to suggest another, they hardly qualify as the pillars of a good and moral life. In almost every case, we can come with up a contrary piece of wisdom. "A stitch in time saves nine," but "Haste makes waste." "The early bird gets the worm," sure enough, but "The second mouse gets the cheese." In the figure of Don Quixote's traveling companion, Cervantes gave us a lovable prototype of the circularity of thinking in proverbs. For every situation and its opposite, Sancho Panza was ready with an ancestral refrain. He is the example par excellence of cloaking novelty with clichés, unlike the mad *caballero* who was completely absorbed in living the freshness of each moment in the world he had concocted for himself.

As you will have guessed by now, to make sense of these

pages, you may need to put on the same pair of glasses I am wearing as I write them. One lens should be ground to detect your image of a truly civil person; the other, to open a window on your memories of genuine civility in action. These may not be your accustomed reading glasses, but I warn you the text will get bleary and the meaning garbled if you read on without them. Not that I intend to appeal to any wisdom higher than we both can access. Nor do I intend to rely on insights any deeper than what each of us can discover with a little time spent reflecting on our lives. All of us know that no philosophy and no sacred teaching is immune from the damage they can cause in the wrong hands and minds. Lacking such a common foundation, of course, there is a constant risk that what I am writing and what you are reading are not always the same thing. Still, as long as they coincide from time to time, as long as a memory is stirred here and there that leads you to join in the praise of civility in general and give a thought to cultivating its pursuit in the things of your life, that is enough.

Three

Some years ago, a scholar-monk from Canada was visiting our home and we were talking about the after-effects of making judgments on the spur of the moment. After a round of confessions, some of them comical and others rather distressing, he tilted his head upwards and fell silent for a few moments. I can still see him sitting in the easy chair to my right as he smiled and began to recount a story he had heard during his training in the monastery about the celebrated Rinzai monk of eighteenth-century Japan, Hakuin.

The story begins with Hakuin returning to Shōin-ji temple from a lengthy tour of monasteries around the country. His monks were glad to see their learned abbot again and the townsfolk were delighted to have their renowned spiritual guide back in their midst. While he was away, a young girl whom he had been teaching to read and write at the temple school got drunk one night and yielded her virtue to a young carpenter from the village. The following day she felt remorse and tried to erase the whole sordid memory. As often happens, nature disagreed. In time it was obvious to the family that she was with child. Her father was irate and demanded to know who the father was, but she kept her secret, fearing for the welfare of the carpenter.

As it happened, a few days before Hakuin's return the girl gave birth to a baby boy. Aware of her father's great respect for Hakuin, she thought that identifying the holy abbot as the father would calm him down. Quite the opposite. He spread word around town about the disgrace his daughter had suffered. Later he led an entourage of the villagers to the monastery, where he hammered on the doors, demanding to see the abbot. Hakuin arrived in the company of the entire community of monks, anxious to know what all the ruckus was about.

"You, Reverend Abbot, have molested my daughter and shamed our family. From now on, the baby is yours to care for," he said as he held out the infant.

"Is that so?" replied Hakuin and took the swaddled newborn into his arms. He withdrew into the monastery, where he took care of the child as if he were his own. Seated in the meditation hall or carrying out his temple duties, Hakuin carried the infant with him everywhere. Even when he went into town to collect alms, he rang his bell and chanted his sutra with the baby in one arm. To the jeers of the villagers, "Hypocrite, deceiver, embarrassment!" he would only bow lightly and reply, "Is that so?"

In short time the young girl could no longer suffer the separation from her child and confessed the truth to her father. That night, when the rest of the town was asleep, the two of them made their way to the monastery gate and called out softly, "Reverend Abbot, Reverend Abbot."

Moments later they could see a lamplight moving down the hallway and out to the courtyard where they were waiting. Hakuin stood there in his nightshirt, the infant still in his arms, as the father lowered his head and began to speak.

"My daughter has lied to both of us. The child is not yours but that of a local artisan. I deeply regret my role in all of this and promise to respect her wishes if you would only return the baby."

Hakuin smiled. "Is that so?" he said, and immediately handed the baby over to the waiting embrace of its mother.

Hakuin is credited with having introduced the *kōan* system into Zen training in Japan. Those who undertake the discipline soon learn that the riddles are not an end in themselves that can be forgotten once they have been answered to the satisfaction of one's spiritual guide. They are a way to train the mind to think clearly, to see the *kōan* in the events of life when others press you to make up your mind as quickly as they have rushed to make up theirs.

All questions of monastic training, religious affiliation, and narrative varnish aside, something in us wants to know, Where was Hakuin standing when he did what he did and said what he said? And how do I get there?

When Hakuin accepted the judgments of his accusers calmly and without defending himself, he showed a trust in the power of the truth that most of us reserve for heady discussions about the place of human nature in the grand cosmic scheme of things. As a strategy for getting through life from day to day it seems more than a little unrealistic. We need to trust our own powers of thought and the efficacy of swift judgment to preserve the social order and our place in it. But there are also times when turning our thoughts into judgments gets in the way. Hakuin did what had to be done without thinking of apportioning blame, allowing everything to collect in his mind and waiting for the truth to out. By abstaining from taking sides, even from taking his own side, he made time for the pieces of the story to fall together and ensure that nothing important was lost along the way.

Imagine what would have happened if he had done what you and I might have done in his sandals, denying the allegations from the start. Some of the townspeople would have taken sides with him and others with the girl's father. Rumor and animus would have taken over and compounded the division. Even if the facts of the matter had eventually been revealed, the father and daughter would have turned on one another in the meantime. Both would have been shamed in the eyes of the villagers and monks, as would those who had taken the charges at face value; and the baby would forever be stigmatized as a symbol of the whole sordid affair. Hakuin took the responsibility on himself—not for something he did but for the whole collection of relationships in need of repair. At the time, his simple "Is that so?" must have seemed the height of vanity or at least an unfeeling detachment from what was going on. But once the child was back with its mother, his words took on a larger meaning. The pressing need to punish the guilty party opened a path to forgiveness and the restoration of harmony within the family and among the villagers. Because he abstained from his own judgment, everyone involved was able, in time, to see through their own judgments. Civility is all about making time to think collectively and trusting in our human capacity for truth.

The example of Hakuin and the young girl with child is moving because it is uncomplicated. The many complex situations we face in life where an "Is that so?" would only make matters worse do not provide that same kind of archetypal clarity. They make us mistrust it. We would rather blunder through with our judgments, backing up and apologizing where we must, but never without a new judgment to replace the one just discarded. Standing naked without an opinion in a time of conflict, life teaches us, is a sign of weakness. Still, I venture to suggest that you have had experiences not unlike Hakuin's, and that it is because of those memories you allow yourself, at least for a moment, to be moved by his poise and civility under pressure.

Someone cuts you off in line and before you can express your righteous anger for all to hear, you see that it is the husband of a dear friend and hold your tongue. The next time someone cuts you off, perhaps you think twice before reacting, but if you do not take the time to think about why you react the way you do, and why you think the thoughts that come to you, soon enough you will be back to your own ways and minor disturbances will once again get treated with the same categorical, generic judgments as the genuinely complex predicaments you get tangled up in. Civility can never become second nature if you just shuffle away from your own failures of judgment without a second thought.

It is not enough to reflect on our second-nature, snap-judgment incivilities when we are alone with ourselves on a long walk through the woods or sipping a glass of wine before the fireplace. We need to be aware when we are in the thick of it. You are standing in an elevator and the person in front of you takes a step back to make room, inadvertently landing a shoe on your foot. You grimace. But what do you do next? You might accuse the person of not watching where they are going, and with that you have stepped on their foot and the foot of everyone else around you. You might also simply ignore the discourtesy. Or you might pull your foot back and whisper an apology to the offender, taking the responsibility on yourself, but also leaving open the possibility that the one to blame might realize their thoughtlessness without any public embarrassment.

There is something else you can do: you can watch how you react. You spontaneously feel the urge to discredit the guilty and credit yourself as an innocent victim, but it only takes a moment to see the fuller picture. A small group of strangers thrown together for a short time, each of them wrapped up in their own thoughts, were anticipating a certain order and harmony to the short ride in the elevator. Your urge was to transform a minor breach of courtesy into a litigation over right and wrong, victim and perpetrator. You abstain and order is restored. Or perhaps you watch yourself and realize that your immediate reaction was to abstain from judging and grudging altogether and simply let the discourtesy pass. Just taking that moment to look at your reaction might bring a smile to your lips: you have just been wrapped up in the embrace of civility. It isn't a matter of taking credit for something you did or didn't do. Something in human nature took over and you did not stand in its way. That something is what makes us social beings and keeps our individual identities from fracturing the harmonious humdrum of everyday life any more than we need to.

The thing about snap judgments is not just that they are so often wrong and made with too little relevant information, but that the need to judge often seems so self-evident. It is as if a binary code had seeped into our behavior and taken over.

I am reminded of something I read twenty-five years ago in Robert Pirsig's *Zen and the Art of Motorcycle Maintenance*. The author, who made a living writing technical computer manuals, challenged the silliness of thinking that there are only two states in a computer, a voltage for one and a voltage for zero, when there is obviously a third stage: unplugged.

This is what Hakuin understood about judging, namely, that there are times when it is not a matter of seeing one's way to a clear judgment but of removing judgment from the picture altogether. Like the thirteenth-century philosopher Dōgen, he rejected the dichotomy between thinking before you act and not thinking. We are taught to use our heads and not just to trust our habits and instincts if we want to be lead a good life. Our education at home and school encourages us not to lose our heads but to approach difficulties in life with our heads screwed on. But Dōgen cut through the line between thinking and not-thinking by stressing the value of doing without thinking. To be alert to those times when thinking and judging get in the way is not foolish or irrational or indecisive. Vigilance over the powers and limitations of reason is foundational for civility. It is as accessible as taking a moment, in the thick of it, to observe how you react, and then to rub your eyes and have another look at what is going on around you.

So many conflicts in life, from the smaller annoyances to the larger discontents, call on us take control and impose our will—even when we have not taken the time to understand what is really going on. Generic thinking is impatient for results and risks trampling on the innocent; collective thinking is hesitant and risks failure to address the urgency of a situation. This is the point, you may think, for prudence to step on the scene to bring a balance to the way we handle ourselves from one end of the spectrum to the other. I think not. To understand what civility exacts of us, we need first to strengthen its spine and set aside the bias that it means appearing irresolute, faint-hearted, bland, and morally anemic. Hakuin was not being prudent or well-balanced in accepting the calumny of the townspeople and the care of the infant they had so readily cast aside. He stood in a position of strength that those who could not see as clearly as he mistook for weakness.

Civility is not the acquisition of a certain fund of knowledge or a certain capacity for good judgment. It is an art that needs practice and refinement. When it sees the strength of human nature in action, it races to know where such a person is standing and to see what the world looks like from there. Its goal is not heroic valor but the discovery of an everyday place from which to act naturally and trust in the received wisdom about being kind to one another. Civility's goodness does not rest with its being recognized as good. For the most part, its goodness is not even apparent to those involved. Its very transparency is testimony to how natural it is at its best.

Some years back, a friend from Spain told me of a story she had heard as a girl about a peasant who found a large, beautiful gem on the side of a road. He picked it up and was admiring its beauty when an unscrupulous merchant passed by and convinced the man that he had lost it, demanding that it be returned to him at once. Without hesitation the man handed the gem over and wished him well. The merchant mounted his horse and rode off chuckling to himself at the peasant's gullibility and thinking how lucky he had been to come upon a treasure that would take care of his financial woes for the rest of his life. Some time later down the road, he drew himself erect in the saddle and abruptly turned around to retrace his path. When he reached the peasant, he dismounted and threw himself at the man's feet.

"Friend, I have come to ask you for something larger, more precious and more useful to me than the splendid gem you just gave me."

"And what is that?" asked the peasant.

"I want to know what made you give it to me."

Our sympathy for the merchant's question goes deeper than any wish to imitate the peasant's simplemindedness in rewarding deception and forfeiting a treasure. Rather, it makes us want to retrace our steps and ask new questions of our own: What made you bear the slander and help the innocent child? What made you apologize to me when it was I who stepped carelessly on your foot? What made you bow to the old woman who told you off in front of everybody? What made you refuse my gratitude until I might repeat the same kindness to others?

To those who value standing their ground and not being taken advantage of, questions like these are worthless. To those who know the power of civility and its deep roots in what is best about us as human beings, the answer's value is beyond the measure of the grandest and most precious stone. The devaluation of civility is subtle but so common we often mistake it for purity of mind and will. We are offended or see an offense committed, and the "natural reaction" is to condemn the injustice and put an end to it—assuming that is what any good person would do in those circumstances. We imagine that by assigning incivility to others, we have somehow made ourselves civil. Once again, the sharp and uncompromising incision of right from wrong blocks us from seeing what Hakuin saw and the others did not: that you do not have to be right to be right. I invite you to pause with me and consider the consequences of this simple idea.

By now you may have tired of my sideswipes at generic thinking, and the way I have been relying on it to move my description of civility along. The fallacy of churning categorical judgments out of legends and anecdotes must seem too obvious to ignore, particularly when the aim is to recommend a kind of non-generic, collective thinking grounded in the concrete interactions of everyday life. Nor will the irony be lost on you that in order to explain myself, I have no choice but to ascend still higher into the clouds of abstraction until we come to a paradox coiled up in the innermost recesses of the mind: the only way to break the hold of fixed ideas over the flux and novelty of the world as we experience it is to set your feet firmly in the idea that the hold needs breaking. Without such a generic idea about the limits of generic ideas, a principle about the limits of principles, a categorical judgment about the limits of categorical judgments, the mind comes to think of itself as a mirror reflecting the things of life to you just as they are. As a result, the pre-judgments you need to filter your consumption of experience and regulate the way you talk about it to others do their work in the background, far from the menacing glare of self-reflection.

Genuine civility can only inhabit a mind that is flexible enough to recognize the nature of generic thinking. Scraps of folk wisdom that advise us to stop and smell the roses, or not to be a know-it-all, or to become like a little child, skirt around the edges of something so fundamental—and, yes, generic—that there is no understanding it without taking the time to watch our mind at work in its own self-important, choosy, distorted, muddled judgments about the things of life. That watching, I am convinced, is the one thing that keeps the particular brew of the rational and the irrational that make up our "thoughts" reasonable.

The hodgepodge of stories and memories I have been stringing together here are tied at one end to this pursuit of detachment from fixed ideas and, at the other, to a pursuit of the conditions in which civility can flourish naturally and without the interference of codes of ethics or norms of etiquette and proper decorum. I have no wish for them to be read for their "moral" or in order to extract some life "lesson" from each of them. Just the opposite. To translate these anecdotes into universal maxims for behavior risks derailing a more genuinely individual reaction to them and rushing to categorical judgments. I have no doubt that such maxims are important, as are codes of morality and an education in courtesy. Civility is different. It works more like an instinctual response to very specific circumstances, an instinct refined by a disposition to selfless kindness but not controlled by an overriding sense of duty or a categorical judgment about what is proper or improper, right or wrong.

I beg you not to rush ahead and counter with situations where it would be impractical or downright stupid to do what any of these examples suggests you do. It is more important that you allow yourself for a moment to be lost in the story and the natural, unaffected civility that holds it together. If there is insight to be had, it is more symbolic than axiomatic. By that I mean that it is a kind of half truth that presses for completion by thinking of a time in your life—the more recent, the better—in which you *could* have acted in the same spirit, spoken the same words, or thought the same thoughts, and imagining what a difference it would have made if you had. This process of "throwing together" (sym-bolizing) a tale you have been told from the life of another and the tale you tell of your own life is the best way—in the end, perhaps the only way—you have of tempering your instincts into habits of civility you can rely on.

The tempering of instinct through hindsight is not our usual way of taking in archetypal stories. The easier course is to stereotype them as inspirational episodes and promptly store them away for some future counsel that we know in our heart we will never seek. This was exactly how it was for me with the legend of Saint Francis recounted in an earlier chapter. It was a story I knew from my youth but had never really understood until a few months ago.

For the past couple of years, we have been hosting a small tribe of stray cats in our garden. We took turns feeding them until the males warmed up to us and regularly scampered to greet us as at the back door as we came and went. One night as we were sitting in the living room after supper, someone drew attention to a scratching sound at the full-length windows that opened out onto the patio. We drew back the curtains and found two of the cats clawing at the screen. Alarmed at the damage they had done with their claws, we shooed them away and returned to our chairs wondering what was to be done. I suggested we contact the city authorities and ask for help to dispose of the whole lot of them. The expense of replacing the screens made it seem the logical thing to do.

The next morning I contacted the office of animal control and was told how to proceed. When I brought the matter up at supper that night, someone who obviously knew more about cats than I objected. It had not even occurred to me that the cats should be part of the decision until she sided with them. She explained that cats need to scrape their claws for all sorts of reasons and that if we would only give them a scratching post or some such surface to rub their paws on, they would leave the screens alone. This is just what we did, and the cats have left the screens alone ever since. With that, I put the matter out of mind. Then, a few days later the name of Francis of Assisi was invoked in discussion and the legend of the wolf of

Gubbio came rushing back to me. What had been no more than inspirational legend was transformed at once into an archetypal image of civility towards animals. The failure to consult a truth that I had known from my youth but which had actually been no more than an inspirational stereotype was too plain to ignore. If you are thinking there must be a lot more of this going on between the lines of the anecdotes I have selected for these pages, you would be right. But none of that is as vital to the praise of civility as what you yourself do to fill up these half truths with the story you tell of your own life.

I apologize if I have left the impression that civility is best practiced with docility, resignation, submissiveness, complacency, and a certain artificiality that does its best not to make waves. My intention was to suggest that there is something in civility that makes it more than just the absence of incivility. Incivility is always something one *does*, whether by letting habit take over, or by a deliberate choice to act or refuse to act. Civility cannot be measured by the incivilities you don't act out, by the judgments you don't pass, by the impolite reactions you renounce. Civility at its heart is not about *you* at all. It is about reading an environment in which you are a participant, and about the harmonious impulses in that environment that can better alleviate the disharmony if you remove yourself from the center. Granted, not all situations allow for this withdrawal from direct confrontation or the temporary surrender of generic thinking based on your personal beliefs. I am talking about those that do.

Getting caught up in an unexpected shift from a harmonious environment to an antagonistic one, where tempers rise and ripple outwards like a pebble dropped into the calm waters of a pond, upsets your balance. Your natural reaction is to secure your own footing and prepare to defend your position. A spectrum of possible responses opens up before you. From one extreme, you can listen to the call of the wild and capitulate to your self-defensive reflexes. From the other, you can beat the quickest path to retreat. Despite the tensions, both responses—as well as any in between—are smooth sailing as long as generic thinking keeps a firm hand on the rudder.

The way of civility is to take a step back from the instinct of self-preservation and take a fuller, more collective look at the environment that has, for the moment, fallen into disarray. This simple act of distancing oneself from the point of contention makes it easier to locate the cornerstone among the rubble. In the case of Hakuin's conflict with the villagers, it was the welfare of the child; with the damaged window screens, it was the cats' need to clean their claws by scratching on something. I was fortunate that someone alerted me to the folly of giving in to my initial reflex to protect my property; Hakuin knew better.

Having an eye for the cornerstone is our way of monitoring the guidelines we live by, lest they fossilize and curdle our ability to make the kinds of moral decisions that depend on them, to know when to impose them and when to hold our hand. To put it more abstractly, no categorical imperative is worthy of human society unless it is accompanied by a categorical understanding about the good sense, common decency, and civility of applying it. Knowing when it's time to be an artist and when it's time to be a moralist is essential to the practice of civility. So, too, is knowing that even the most categorical of moral judgments must not be made in isolation. Collective thinking is not a rejection of the need to challenge the habits of others, but only of the need to impose our conscience on others egregiously.

To assign different degrees of incivility to others and imagine that this make us civil is such a widespread form of self-deception that it is almost culturally acceptable. It belongs to the more general tendency to make reciprocity and negotiation the predominant model of human interaction, and to make being right the predominant model of civic responsibility. You don't always have to be right to be right, just as you don't always have to be truthful to tell the truth. Being civil might seem to imply being dishonest with those close to us who expect us to be more forthright with them than with total strangers. There is something cold and unfeeling about being polite rather than truthful.

Obviously, not all situations matter the same. When a friend asks about a particularly hideous sweater they just bought, "How do you like it?," only a fool would think a frank answer mattered more than their friend's feelings. That is common sense. But now suppose a stranger is rude to me, but rather than accuse them, I simply acknowledge the insult, without sarcasm, and hold my peace. It ends there. I wasn't right because it was my fault; I was right because the mistake was acknowledged and corrected without anyone having to take the blame. Defusing gives the other party a chance to recognize their fault. Whether they do so or not is not important, but if I judge them at once, I diminish that chance and invite altercation. You might think to yourself, If I let everybody cut me off, I'd never get where I need to get. This is the fallacy of turning what was only a minor inconvenience into a debate over universal principles of proper behavior. The problem is not having principles or making generalizations, both of which are emotionally charged. It's trampling over *other* feelings in the environment to get there.

In a sense, civility is the quest of the invisible, the inaudible. We may try to forget about it during our assault on things that don't conform to our expectations in order to protect our private interests. But it's there, in the deepest recesses of our desire for realizing what is best in our humanity, waiting to be discovered.

There are things in the shadows and between the lines that only surface when you close your eyes, give them a good rub to wipe away your expectations, and then open them again to re-collect your surroundings. Civility begins with seeing things that ordinary politeness and good manners, and our bias about their limits, too often pass over. Not making snap judgments before taking a good look is hard enough. Not making snap judgments about those who make snap judgments about you, without pausing to listen to what is not being said and seeing what is not immediately apparent through all the clutter, is harder still. But that is precisely what the praise of civility looks like in practice.

Four

By now you must think we are going around in circles. I confess, I am unable to find a straight line from a simple intuition to a full-throated praise of civility. Part of this is due to my unrepentant reliance on stories and anecdotes, although it is probably not very different from the way most of us tend to rely on stories and anecdotes to guide us in dealing with thoughtless and insulting behavior or other unforeseen interruptions to the flow of our lives. All things considered, offering alternative examples seems the more powerful logic for making a case as simple and straightforward as the one I am making here.

What is more, I am not convinced there is any way to "teach" civility in the abstract. My parents—like yours, I suppose—tried to teach me principles to live by. What I learned as a child, however, I learned more from my father's timely but cryptic comments in stressful situations and my mother's unexplainable hospitality towards visitors who intruded into our lives and upset our plans without warning. As I grow older, I am surprised how little guidance I have taken from trying not to repeat their failures as parents, and how much from the things they said or did on certain occasions. To this day, I find putting those memories into words more engaging than any of the rational precepts I carry around with me.

We have been insisting all along that genuine civility is radically selfless, and for that reason have focused on the effect it has on others. But in each of the preceding examples, as well as in all of those that follow, there are also important insights to be gained by those who act civilly. My thoughts go immediately to something that happened thirteen years ago during a stay in Europe.

Ueda Shizuteru, a leading Japanese philosopher, had been invited to the Asia center located on the second floor of an old church in the city of Bologna. I accompanied him and his wife, as I had several times before, to serve as a translator. A diverse audience of about sixty people seated on tatami mats listened attentively as he tried to explain the meaning of "nothingness" and relate it to the transition from awakened insight to compassionate practice.

The venerable old professor was no more than twenty minutes into his talk when a small commotion broke out at the back of the room. A man had stood up and was weaving his way in and out of the audience and toward the door. As people were scooting out of the way, many in the audience shrugged their shoulders and grimaced. The puzzled look on their faces was unmistakable. Why would he leave in the middle? Did he find it unintelligible or disagreeable, or was he just bored? And why offend the speaker by walking out? Professor Ueda just smiled and carried on. In a few minutes the mood had calmed and the whole episode was forgotten.

The proceedings concluded with a lively discussion, after which we were served coffee and cakes. The group dispersed within the hour, and I led the Uedas down the staircase and out to the street, where a taxi was waiting to take us back to our hotel. The taxi door was already opened when the man who had mysteriously disappeared during the talk came running toward us. We waited to receive him. It took him a minute to catch his breath before he began to speak.

"As I listened to you, I knew at once that you were the one. For some months I have been holding on to these two jars of oil, the last press from an old and dying olive tree that has been in the family for generations. I had been waiting for someone special to give these to."

He held out the jars with tears in his eyes.

"Please, from my heart. They belong to you."

The Uedas bowed silently to the man, whose name we never learned, until he turned and walked away. We stepped into the cab and returned to the hotel without a word. I could sense how deeply the professor and his wife were moved, but we never spoke of it again. Perhaps they felt, as I did, that anything we might say would be superfluous—or, as the Japanese saying goes, like putting a roof on a roof.

I have recounted this episode numerous times when asked about my fondest memories of the professor and his wife, both since deceased. Only later did I come to think that perhaps there was more to the silence of the Uedas. I had long thought of the gift as a fitting homage to an extraordinary human being, but as I think back on it now, I am certain they received it rather as a homage to the humanity that shone transparently, before their very eyes, through that simple act of giving.

I cannot help wondering how all those furrowed brows that looked disapprovingly at the man as he stumbled over them and out of the lecture hall would have given way to a penitent smile at their own misunderstanding. The bigger question is what was going on in the man himself. I have no way of knowing, but from the way the man distanced himself immediately from the scene, I imagine the emotion of the moment must have brought him that sense of happiness that comes from letting go. Like me, I am sure you have known the inexpressible delight of parting with something of great personal significance to you to someone whom you consider just the right person. To them, it may seem no more than a trifle, but to you, it is no less than part of yourself and you feel more fully yourself for having done so.

If we think of civility only in terms of conflict resolution, Professor Ueda and the jars of olive oil may seem out of place. But the gesture of giving without expecting anything in return is the very lifeblood of civility and reinforces our capacity to act more civilly in the face of the incivility of others when the need arises. The normal requirements of a transaction are out of place. The very thought of exchange or retribution would shatter the enchantment of being caught up in the coincidence of the offer and the reception. Civility is always about coincidence. It is not a relationship you step into voluntarily and then step out of. It is something you fall into, like falling in love.

We might as well be straightforward about it. Civility is a form of love. Loving another or being loved back are the effects of being in love, not the cause. So, too, civility is not just a skill we engage to solve problems, but a medium that engages what is best in us, whether or not there is a problem to be solved. Taken all together, what goes on in that medium is not only a matter of my *being civil* but also of my *being in civility*.

Again, if we think of civility as an event that surrounds and entwines those "involved," then we ourselves are as much affected by acting civilly as those we interact with. So, too, our incivility to others taints the whole environment and us with it. Civility happens, and it would probably happen a lot more if we just got out of the way until it was clear that we were needed. Just to be able to recognize when you have become an obstacle to civility rather than its carrier is already half the battle. When there is really nothing you can do but complain about how helpless you are, silence may be the best response. The fact is, refusing to think of yourself as the victim of what is an obvious offense against civility can clear your head and help you stop things from going any further than they already have.

To the point, I would like to recount a legend about the ninth-century caliph Al-Ma'mūn of Baghdad and his beautiful Arabian horse. A tribesman had his heart set on purchasing it, but the caliph would not budge. Knowing Al-Ma'mūn to be a kind man, the tribesman devised a way to trick him. He disguised himself as a sick beggar and stretched out along the side of a road he knew the caliph would take. Sure enough, Al-Ma'mūn happened by, dismounted, and offered to carry him to a nearby inn where he could be cared for. No sooner had he lifted the sickly stranger up onto his horse than the tribesman sat upright and galloped off. Al-Ma'mūn chased after him on foot, calling out to him to stop. When he had reached a safe distance, the tribesman turned his horse around.

"You have stolen my horse," Al-Ma'mūn shouted to him, "but I have a favor to ask. Do not tell anyone what you've done."

"And why should I not?" asked the thief, smiling.

"Because someday there may be a man lying on the roadside who is really ill and could use the help of a passer-by. If word gets out how you tricked me out of my horse, no one will dare stop."

Before you catch yourself snickering at how unrealistic and simple-minded it would be actually to try and imitate the kindly caliph in a modern urban setting, stop for a moment and think what a grace it would be to find the place where he was standing and see what it was he saw. Rather than following his first impulse to reclaim what was rightfully his and bring justice to bear on the one who had swindled him, his first thoughts went to protecting trust in the deeper human impulse of people to give a hand to those in need. That ability to see through the surface to what is more important is an art that no amount of training in proper manners or of education in ethical principles can replace. Before you can ever hope to practice it in times of conflict, you have first to learn to let go of possessions you hold dear in order to honor the things that really matter.

When you are treated uncivilly, protecting others from being infected should be your first priority. If your first thought is to defend yourself, chances are you will get caught up in a situation where one party can only win by the other party losing. The civil thing is to identify the disharmony as the real problem and to realize that apportioning blame or proclaiming innocence can only cement the opposing sides in place and delay the restoration of harmony.

To repeat, not all incivility needs to be forgiven on the spot and glossed over for the sake of calmer tempers. There are things in life that ought to infuriate us and against which we ought to revolt—and, yes, to do so in the name of what is best in our humanity. My point is to underline the rude shock of discovering how often and how unnecessarily we carry thoughts about those extreme cases over into what are really banal and entirely digestible bits of indecent behavior on the part of others. We would be impoverished as human beings if we did not carry around with us at least the hope of standing up to tyranny with courage. We are no less impoverished by mistaking ordinary acts of dim-witted, ill-mannered, hot-headed, low-minded thoughtlessness as generic acts of tyranny.

The ability to see through the surface of things without losing sight of the surface does not come easily. We all know how to look at the flowers printed on a thin curtain and then look through the curtain to the flowers growing in the garden. When it comes to seeing through a disturbance unexpectedly thrown into our faces, our trusted recipes for response keep us from seeing behind appearances or listening to what is not being said. We expect things to unfold as they have unfolded before, and to know just what to do about it. We look and do not see; we hear and do not listen. Everything collapses into the cowardly demand for swift judgment; there is not even time to recognize ourselves in those we judge. Turn your back and walk away, if you will. Or step in and get involved. Unless you can see through the fog and hear through the noise to what you share with both sides of the conflict, nothing you do or do not do measures up to the courage to be civil.

Among the many legends reconstructed from historical scraps to tell the story of Prince Siddhartha's experience of becoming buddha (awakened), there is one that has to do specifically with seeing through the fog. After an exhausting but fruitless period of rigorous asceticism, he sat himself down beneath a Bo tree, determined not to get up until he was to be delivered from ignorance. During that time he was tempted three times by the lord demon of the senses, Māra, and each time he looked intently until he could see through the veil of appearances. A horde of monsters attacking him with fiery swords were revealed to be flower petals carried by the wind. Next, Māra sent his lovely daughters to seduce him, but Siddhartha waited patiently for them to show themselves as the hideous witches they were. A third time Māra tempted him with doubts about his ability to achieve the wisdom he sought or teach it to others, but the young prince turned to the earth to hold firm and resist his fears.

When Siddhartha at last awakened from the dream of the world of appearances and saw the world for what it is, his first act was to turn to Māra for another look. He immediately recognized the face of the tempter as none other than his own. This act of seeing something and then seeing through it to discover something of yourself, all the time without losing sight of the initial appearance of things, lines the whole complex history of a philosophy grounded in the experience of enlightenment. It is also the quintessence of the art of civility.

Trying to see deeper and to resist the interference of instinct to judge every assault on civility as a variation of the kill-or-be-killed conditions of warfare means becoming part of the *whole* conflict and not just the part that strikes you, the outside spectator, as right. Not being too quick to separate the offender from the offended is not to be stupid or morally paralytic. It is a decision not to judge in order to see more. The true fools are those who genuflect to their principles and refuse to see beyond them. At the same time, to step into the whole is to accept responsibility—to awaken your ability to respond—which is not the same as simply taking action or making up your mind on where to place the blame.

We really do need to rescue the word *responsibility* from its captivity to the idea of atonement, indemnity, recompense, or redress imposed on the guilty in the name of the innocent. Taking responsibility for what you do, we are told from childhood, is a sign of maturity; refusing to take responsibility, a sign of cowardice and selfishness. There are two problems with this way of thinking, one of them obvious and easy to adjust to, the other upsetting in the extreme.

First, it forgets about the things *we* do, as a family, a community, a nation, an earth. As obvious a part of a responsible life as this is, the temptations to dissociate oneself from personal accountability for a group's actions are many and often victorious.

Second, hitching responsibility only to one's own actions quickly forgets about shouldering any obligation to repair damage that you had no part in. Where this gets particularly demanding is when it has to do with something that only you can do: accept responsibility for what others have done to you, erase all blame from the picture, and answer for the effects without resentment or hostility.

The reality is often very different. It's an old story

and one we have all heard again and again. A young girl dreams of being a ballerina or a doctor, but her parents will not support her. She leaves home as soon as she is old enough to go out on her own, where she struggles to make a living and begin a family of her own. But in her heart, she bears the memory like a festering sore that cracks open whenever she speaks of what happened to her. "If it weren't for them, I would have...." The blame for what was done to her makes her incapable of responding to the hurt and changing her story. She thinks it a sin too grave to be forgiven, but really, it's a wound that will not heal because she is fixed on her parents' failure to accept the blame for her life.

The response of the good caliph Al-Ma'mūn who was bested by the horse thief is a paradigm of accepting full responsibility for what others have done to you rather than flail about in search of someone else to hold accountable for the way you are. Handing oneself over to the simple instinct to respond to an injury without having first to decide who inflicted it and how they are to be held accountable is a revelation of our native disposition to civility

As examples and illustrations of the case for civility continue to pile up and overlap each other, you may already have begun to expect a sharper profile to just what we are talking about—if not a clean-cut definition, then at least the consolation of having its main attributes arranged in

some kind of logical order. But I have come to praise civility, not to bury it. I stand by my decision to avoid academic questions of ethics and morality and will let my thoughts scurry along freely on the heels of the anecdotes that keep these pages stitched together.

Most of us hold the ability to make judgments without prejudice in high esteem and only wish we were better at it. We tend to think of prejudices as a sign of sloppy thinking and forget about the possibility of cultivating them as something we cannot get along without. For example, you may have a few friends from another region or country you have never visited and be so enamored of them that you automatically carry around a cheery idea of their whole country. But then you meet someone else from the same place who is distasteful or insolent. Your cheery idea is deflated at once. This happens to us all the time, but we rarely pause to pay it attention. We just exchange one set of judgments for another and leave our affection for generic comparison unquestioned, as strong as ever.

Think of our words, those little units of prejudice we rely on. We know what to call most of the things around us because someone decided on their "names" and recorded them in books for settling disputes on how language is passed on. This may all seem very objective, but it is anything but objective. Where we set the contours to separate one item in the world from another is more a matter of convention than we may realize. The five senses would seem to lift us up above our local culture and its way of experiencing the world and talking about it, but much of the time it is our culture and language that lifts us up above the bodily senses. Even our perception and imagination of the surrounding world is a function of prejudice. Or, to put it still more radically, even our efforts to see the world without prejudging it and to talk about it in culturally neutral language—the goal of what we call the "natural sciences"—are colored by our notion of objectivity and the way we brandish those prejudices over the heads of those who see the world with different eyes.

I do not mean to twist our everyday commonsense into knots and make us feel more helpless in dealing with our prejudices than we already do. My only point is that we couldn't even process the ordinary data of our eyes and ears without a bedrock of expectations born of the memory of data we have processed in the past. We could not talk about colors or tables and chairs or trees and animals if we did not already have some expectation of how to sort our perceptions of them. And that, I repeat, is ordinary, everyday, essential prejudice.

(Admittedly, most of us have a certain "prejudice" against seeing prejudice as something useful or necessary. By itself, the very mention of the word seems to burrow itself into conscience and arouse our disapproval. Much as I dislike the wholesale prejudice against prejudice, I am not so foolish as to suppose the word can be rehabilitated by logic alone. If you find it offensive, I suggest replacing it with the more neutral term "prejudgment," a benefit of writing in English that is not the case with most European languages.)

The prejudice most of us associate with the word is a side effect of this most natural need of a working mind. It is the evaluation we attach to things to keep them distinct. In the same way that shape and color and light all help us keep the name of a chair distinct from the name for the table, even though both are lumped together as furniture, we make a distinction between the things we like and value and the things we dislike and devalue. The names of things are fairly stable in a community speaking the same language and fit nicely into dictionaries. They are a pillar of social harmony. But the way we classify our likes and values is fluid, changeable, personal. These prejudices need cultivating, not by hardening them but by keeping them soft, open to change and surprise. When prejudices about likes and values become stiff, they easily get weaponized and are no longer of any use to the pursuit of social harmony. Of course, we cannot live without stiffening our judgments into habits of thought. To do so would leave us defenseless at worst and irresolute, mediocre persons at best. Cultivating prejudices about the things that matter requires that we think twice about judgments that make us uneasy when we pass them.

Having prejudices as a matter of necessity does not mean lionizing them or letting them grow wild. As I was growing up, and long thereafter, I was often told I had to learn to listen more closely to others before deciding too quickly what I think they are trying to say. The people who told me that were right, but I only understood what they meant when I learned to listen to myself. Paying attention to your own language at work is simpler than you might think, but also a far side more frightening. If you are like me, you will find the memory of things you said during the day will stay with you to the evening in surprising detail. Words spoken in jest and in seriousness, in joy and in pain, things said to strangers and friends, to family and shopworkers, questions asked or questions answered, remarks profound or flippant—the whole jumble of things that make up our daily verbiage is a window to the prejudices about what we value and what we like.

Monitoring your language as if you were an outside observer on the lookout for usage deemed unacceptable by society is like fighting prejudice with prejudice, judging one set of judgments with another. This is how language gets flattened out and loses its texture and layers. Before we begin to police hurtful language or change expressions that marginalize minority values, we need to be conscious of our own language. Before you discover what your prejudices are, before you identify the values and preferences that you communicate to others on the surface or between the lines of the language you use, you cannot really decide which ones are proper and which not.

St. Augustine is said to have been grateful that he was not responsible for his dreams, but he was also hounded by the thought, "Surely it cannot be that when I am asleep I am not myself." Would you hold someone accountable if they used a racial slur word in a dream or when talking in their sleep? We may decide at some point to hold ourselves accountable for these seemingly uncontrollable outbursts, but it is ours to judge and ours alone. But even when we are not physically asleep, we are often in a kind of half-awake stupor when we catch ourselves in a hurtful prejudice. The important thing is to wake up—not to adjust to norms but to give ourselves a good shaking. Things we were taught before we had the critical sense to reject them sometimes just slip out. It is one thing for me to look at this; for others to condemn me for my slips is often no more than an unproductive incivility that puts me on the defensive where it is harder to stop and look.

To repeat: we cannot live without prejudice. Life is too short to examine everything we say. This much is obvious. Nevertheless, there are blocks of prejudice, clusters of ideas that need breaking apart. How do we know when a prejudice needs to be dredged up and looked at or when we should just let it be? We know. We always know. The deep, "unconscious" prejudices that form the bedrock of the mind, the coding that lets our minds deal with new perceptions and new information may not be entirely out of reach, but their interference is often too dark and impenetrable to command our attention. But there are also shallow, "preconscious" prejudices that stand just out of view at the fringes of attention. We know them by the shadows they cast over the clarity of our opinions. Their presence is often no more than an inkling, a sense that there is more to see than we are comfortable with seeing.

Who of us has not *known* the bias in our choice of

words or a decision to act in a certain way? We hesitate to admit the meddling of prejudice and purposely snuggle up to it, but we know it's there. We prefer to let the moment pass, comforted by the assurance that it will go back to sleep if we keep it out of view. We listen to stories of kindness, selflessness, and generosity and a small light of recognition goes on. Then it dims and we go back to the less demanding demands of the "real world." Somehow, with certainty, we know that these shadowy, preconscious sentiments that invite us to wrestle with bias would overturn the habits of thought and action we have become accustomed to. I may rant against the prejudices that keep a society or culture divided against itself. I may debate furiously against the bias in an opponent's point of view. I may work tirelessly to scrub the discrimination baked into the ruling ideals or laws or philosophies of the age. But unless I turn my head to face those preconscious inklings at the fringes of my own mind, my words are a sounding brass or a tinkling cymbal. The opposite of prejudice, after all, is not open-mindedness. Open-mindedness is not the absence of all judgment, critical or prejudicial. It is vigilant judgment.

Harsh judgments spoken in haste often punish us more than the person we are criticizing. They leave behind a residue of resentment, and sometime regret, that eats at us. We think of how we might have made our point more sharply, how angry we are at the person we judged. On the one hand, we all know how words can hurt, and we are taught from a young age to be careful what we say. On the other hand, we may not give enough thought to how much they hurt the one who speaks them, whether as a bitter aftertaste or as a mistaken belief that we have to keep up the image we have created for others to see.

Fixed ideas we have of ourselves, ideas that make us feel comfortable, that reconfirm that our world is *the* world, are our way of inoculating ourselves against awareness of our own biases. This is how intellect pushes us into confusing opinion with reality. Curable bias is like a lamp we carry around in the daytime to "show others the way." But the sun is shining, and our lamp will work only if we first turn the world dark. There are biases that we have it in ourselves to correct, even though we often prefer to let them darken the opinions of others. Rather than fight *with* ourselves we fight *for* ourselves.

If prejudice is a necessity, then all the more reason to cultivate habits of judgment. Habits of judgment are not solutions to problems. They are seeds out of which solutions grow. Prejudices are not instincts that can be left alone until they get out of hand. They need tending, just as carpenters need to take time to sharpen their tools. The first step, always the first step, is to accept the grace of those moments when a prejudice wobbles unsteadily into mind and begs for attention. Without that, civility can only feel labored and unnatural.

Five

It should be clear by now that my use of the word "civility" does not coincide with its ordinary sense of good manners and proper decorum, whether heartfelt or a thin veneer of etiquette. The civility I have set out to praise is not an offshoot or side effect of the social mores that control the way we behave in public. Nor is it a set of ethical principles grounded in personal conviction and applied with proper deliberation. It is a state of mind that reveals itself in the natural impulse to reach out with kindness to someone in distress, to soothe the hostilities of the moment and restore harmony, to enjoy the happiness of others. I have no doubt that good manners and moral persuasion have much to contribute to the common good and the quality of life, but their contribution does not cover life wall-to-wall. Their efficacy diminishes before the passions and eccentricities of falling deeply in love. They are equally unreliable as a guide to civility.

At the same time, I have no doubt that civility is for the most part powerless in the face of armed violence, systemic discrimination, mass hysteria, mental derangement, illogical reasoning, and every sort of calculated cruelty we humans are capable of inflicting on one another.

But no catalog of all the things civility cannot do and all the situations in which it is out of place should blind us to everything it can do and all the situations in which it is the better option.

Let us go back for a moment to the experience of falling in love. Civility does not entail the long-term commitment we normally associate with love. It certainly does not share the intense swings from ecstasy to heartache. But this important thing it does share with love: that it is selfless in the here-and-now. It is something you literally "fall into," something larger than yourself, something that suspends the rules of logic or even common sense.

There is an image in a medieval Chinese poem by the celebrated woman poet and calligrapher Guan Daosheng that I find helpful in taking the comparison a step further:

> Taking a lump of clay, I mold an image of you and shape one of myself.
> I take both figures, add a little water, and knead them together into a new lump of clay.
> Then I make two new figures, one of you and one of me.
> Now I am in your clay and you in mine.

Who among us would not wish to have the sentiments of those lines as part of the story of their lives? Even the calmest, most convoluted telling of the ins and outs of love would count the faint memory of such intensity of feeling a blessing never to be forgotten. To have lost oneself and one's beloved, however briefly, in something greater—

does this not tap, in some inscrutable way, into the very marrow of our humanity? And if so, might not the ordinary working of civility we happen into or allow ourselves to be kneaded into remind us of that very impulse that is always just within reach?

When Sigmund Freud gave up his scalpel for a couch (his first published paper, we may recall, had to do with dissecting eels to locate their missing testicles), the only tool he had to rely on was talk. It took him a while to realize it, but it was not *his* talk but the patient's that worked whatever cure there was to be had. A therapist's interpretations of another's memories and fantasies, whatever one may think of their scientific validity, were of no therapeutic consequence until that person was able to retell the story of their life without the anxiety and neurosis that had crippled their storytelling before.

Freud was right on one thing. We are always telling and retelling the story of our lives, and these revisions are a natural attempt by the mind to replace what has been damaged, to dull the pain, or otherwise to restore balance. The same mechanism is at work when we own up to our responsibility as when we lay the blame on others, when we tell the truth about what happened as when we cover it up. Whether we accept the past or repress it, it is still part of the story we tell of our life. Whether expressed overtly in words or clandestinely in anxieties, the memories and dreams, the hopes and the illusions that accumulate from day to day—inflate them or devalue them as we will—are never completely forgotten. In an important sense, I am the sum of the stories I tell about my life. Listening to the stories of other lives, fiction and fact alike, affects the story we tell of our own lives. So, too, does the audience to whom we do the telling. More often than we know, the pieces are being rejumbled like patterns in a kaleidoscope, and with them our perception of who we are and how we want to be perceived. There is no one "true identity" that can judge all the others, just as there is no one true story of your life. We invent ourselves anew each time we tell a story. To our last conscious breath, the whole story is forever in the making. The present is not just the result of everything in the past; it is the permanent homeland of the story we tell about it.

Now the story of our lives writ small also frames our story of humanity writ large. The two stories never quite coincide. There is always a disconnect between who I am and what I think of the human nature I am born into. There is more here than a simple charge of hypocrisy or personal failure can account for. It is a way of locating ourselves in a story greater than our own, and the way we present that story to others has a power that reaches beyond the confines of personal identity.

One of the best images of the way these two stories interact is to be found in the frame story of that eighth-century jewel of Islamic literature known as *One Thousand and One Nights*. It begins one night when King Shahzaman surprises his wife in the arms of a palace slave and puts them both to the sword on the spot. Devastated and ashamed, he goes to visit his brother, King Shahryār. By chance he looks out the palace window and discovers his brother's wife engaged in even more scandalous activity. Unable to contain himself, Shahzaman bares the facts to Shahryār and the two regents set out on a journey to consider their next course of action.

They walk day and night until they come to a meadow by the seashore, where they stop to rest under a tree. Suddenly they see a thick black column of smoke rising up out of the sea. Frightened, they scamper up the tree and watch. The smoke materializes into a genie, who unchains a trunk from which a young woman of splendid proportions emerges. The genie falls asleep and the woman signals the two brothers to approach. She shows them a necklace composed of five hundred and seventy rings whose owners she had bedded without arousing the slightest suspicion in her guardian. After securing their rings for her collection, she takes her leave with the taunt that once a woman puts her mind to something, not even a genie can get in her way.

Shahryār's distrust of his wife deepens and sours his disposition towards women in general. Returning to the palace, he has his wife beheaded and sets in motion a vile plot to ensure that no woman will ever get the better of him again. He orders his vizier to bring him a virgin that night, and every night thereafter, and to have them killed once they have lost their maidenhead. After three years, the supply of virgins in the kingdom was exhausted, save for the two maiden daughters of the vizier, Scheherazade and her younger sister Dunyazad. Hoping to put an end to the cruelty, Scheherazade convinces her father to present her to the king's bed. As the fateful hour approaches, the cunning maiden implores the king to allow her to bid farewell to her sister before she goes to her death. He agrees, and while he steals her innocence, his servants rush off in search of Dunyazad. The two sisters embrace in tears and the younger begs for one last story before they part forever. The king relents and Scheherazade begins to spin her tale. Dawn approaches before she can finish, but the king is so intrigued by the story that he allows her to live another day to hear how it ends.

And so it was, night after night—for a thousand and one nights—Scheherazade weaved her intricate and enchanting adventures, each leaving the king on edge and anxious to know its conclusion. Storytelling was, literally, her way of salvation. It bought her time to preserve her life and cure him of his barbaric ways. For his part, the king was so utterly confused by his jealousy and bedazzled by the stories that he could not even recognize himself in the mirror of Scheherazade's narrations about people saving themselves by telling stories. Her ruse succeeds and at last King Shahryār confesses on the thousand-and-first night that his soul has been powerfully transformed by listening to her. At that point, Scheherazade calls for Dunyazad, who enters with twin infants at the breast and a third crawling on all fours behind her. Scheherazade reminds him of the two occasions she was ill disposed, the times she gave birth to his children. Shahryār calls for his brother Shahzaman and tells him what has transpired. He, too, is healed of his misgivings and later marries Dunyazad.

Scheherazade's use of stories as a way to redeem the king from his condemnation of women is an image of the way two lives can intersect at a place other than the place of the conflict that has them in its grip. I am not talking about scampering off to a moral high ground from which to look down on those left stuck in the mud of their own wickedness. On the contrary, the common ground she sought was only accessible by suspending judgment and rational argument in hope of elevating the conflict above personal interest. In putting her own life at risk, her hope of salvation seems to echo the prayer of the psalmist, "Lead me to a rock that is higher than I."

To follow Scheherazade as she guides the king step by step to a greater measure of his humanity is to understand what happens in ordinary, unpretentious, acts of civility. Civility is not just an act of selflessness; it is a declaration about human nature. It tells the same story about the basic human impulse to conviviality as the anecdotes I have used to illustrate the meaning of civility. No, it does more than that. It testifies to what happens when that impulse is liberated from its ties to personal interests so as to think and act more collectively. By the same token, incivility is more than a casual act of selfishness. It testifies to what happens when that impulse is bound too tightly to the abstract and generic judgments that rush into mind to defend us against an apparent threat to our person or to our expectations of how others ought to act. By keeping myself at the center of events, the stories I tell about humanity are always writ small; my view of humanity is trimmed to coincide with my image of myself.

The native impulse to reach out to others selflessly and cultivate conviviality holds a special place throughout the history of philosophy and religion. The varieties of theory and doctrine in which this common feature of our humanity is honored are evidence of the durability of our trust in this potential to get over ourselves for a greater good. This trust is inevitably shadowed by counterarguments in support of an inherent self-interest or wickedness so bred in the bone of the human condition that it is either indelible or curable only by divine intervention.

Unfortunately, there is no place we can stand to look at our humanity from the outside and make up our minds to trust or distrust its inner promptings. What we can say is that to take a stand in praise of civility as something more fundamental to our essence than the laws or mores or good manners, we need to protect ourselves from darker instincts, to draw the line at describing incivility as the workings of an incurable, "natural" disposition. The counter-impulses to civility and incivility may both be moored in our natures, but the choice to pursue our better side remains. To pull ourselves out of the center of things and retell the story of our lives in more convivial terms entails two different but adjoining choices, one for overarching the story we tell ourselves about our humanity and the other for the multitude of small stories we tell from day to day.

Some years ago I was on a plane en route to my father's funeral, wondering what I was going to say when it was my turn to speak. I remembered a passage I came across as a young graduate student. It was from the eulogy that the fifth-century BCE statesman Pericles delivered to honor the heroes who had died in the Peloponnesian War. I had then, and continue to have, a very low opinion of war as a paradigm for heroism, so I cannot say what possessed me to remember those words, but I did. Had I not been so full of myself and my preoccupations with having something suitable to say at such a somber time, I am sure I would have heard the flutter of wings.

"The whole earth is the sepulcher of great people," Pericles said. "And their stories are not carved in stone and planted in their native soil, but live on far away, often without visible symbol, woven into the stuff of others' lives."

I knew immediately that these were the right words for the occasion. Altogether, I considered my father to have been a great man. And now he belongs to something bigger than his own life and his own family. His story is not something that can be carved on a headstone and planted in a family plot. It will live on in the empty spaces of our conversations, between the lines of our letters, woven into the stuff of our lives.

Woven into the stuff of others' lives. That was the phrase that caught my attention then and comes to mind now as I think about the choice of an enveloping story, a story behind the sum of the stories that makes us who we are. There is not much I have to say about what goes on after death, but this much I do know: who we are is larger than the sum of our days and larger than our death.

How do I know that? And how did Pericles? How could he have been sure that people didn't just simply die and linger in memory until their story faded away, at which point they would die forever? How did he know that their stories would live as long as there is life on the earth? On what did he base his conviction that you cannot bury a life in one place, but that it belongs to the whole of the earth?

The simple answer is, he didn't know, at least not in the way we normally know things. But neither did he simply believe, as if an act of faith could provide him with information that others did not have. What he knew—and what any of us can know, if only we would take the trouble to think about it—is that there is a hope in us, an irrepressible trust that somehow, in one way or other and against all evidence to the contrary, time is on our side. We don't believe this because we choose it, but because it so much a part of our nature that we cannot even call ourselves human without the hope that time is partisan with all that lives and dies.

Look at the evidence. Sooner or later, time makes a mockery of who we once were. We get old, we get sick, our hair thins and falls out, our bodies sag, our teeth go bad, we turn into caricatures of our former selves. No matter what shape we and our doctors keep us in, time *will* turn against us. But that is not the whole of it. The sun rises after the darkness of night, the warm winds of spring melt the winter away year after year, the flower wakes up from its sleep and blooms again. Children grow up and have children of their own, the earth does not forget how to produce food. If time were to stop being good to us, we'd be finished.

Eventually time does stop being good to us—as individuals. We die, and the people we love die. We are left with a choice: either we accept that the desire for time to be good to us is a silly pipe-dream, and that in the end neither the good nor the evil we do lives on after us; or we reaffirm the hope, against all the promptings of reason, that time is on our side.

It's that simple. To be true to the deep and ineradicable human impulse to live as long as we can, we need to hope that the future will remember the life of the past, that no death is large enough to erase anything great that ever lived. However resolutely logic retaliates against such hope, we *need* a way to venerate our trust in the goodness of time. All the concrete expectations of life after death, or of finally rescuing everything that once lived from the curse of death—which differ from one philosophy and religion to the next—are mere idols if they eclipse that simple, deep, universal sentiment of hope that time is on our side. The reason we create those images and believe so fervently in them is that this hope is as vital to us as the air we breathe. Without it, we would not be human at all. It is not that Pericles chose to ignore the evidence of what the war had shown to both sides. He chose not to be controlled by it.

Nothing is ever really forgotten, perhaps not remembered in the way I remember it, perhaps not even in a human way at all—but everything *is* remembered. We learn how to forget, knowing full well that we cannot change the past. We reconstruct it around the events on which we choose to hinge our identity and the events from which we prefer to unhinge ourselves. But the miracle of connectivity, which all the laws of the cosmos presuppose, is that nothing and no one, and none of the marks they make, is detachable from the whole. In the words of the poet Karthika Naïr, "Some ties stay unsevered, even when tattered." Symbols of this connectivity are embedded in the myths as old as recorded history that speak of reward and punishment in the afterlife. And these symbols draw on that fundamental human impulse to belong to a grander story, a vast loom on which the stories of all our lives are woven together.

I realize that whatever I say about the choice to trust in the fundamental orientation of our nature to conviviality is both too much and too little. Too much, because its conclusion is so expansive and shaped more by sentiment than objective reason. Too little, because the assertions are so vaguely expressed and remote from the vivid language of ordinary experience. The only proof I can offer is that trust is possible, and that the consequences of losing it are monstrous. In the end, everything hangs on how that trust affects the way we choose to relate to others and the way the stories we relate about those choices accumulate over time and express themselves in the habits that carry our identity from one day to the next. The beliefs about human nature we affirm in the truth at large are only as alive as the choices we make in the particular.

I have been insisting in a general way that what marks civility off from good behavior or proper manners is that it is somehow a conscious choice and at the same time a habit of acting naturally. Habits are necessary, but they are not necessarily autonomic reactions to think or behave in a certain way. It is by habit that we rely on the predictability of generic thinking. Habits are our way of keeping the mind afloat in the stream of "everything flows." Civility begins where those habits begin to crack or unravel. What we have been calling collective thinking is the cradle of a wisdom that is never merely habitual, a wisdom that comes to light when circumstances cry out for more than habit. I have loaded these pages with concrete examples of this wisdom in action, but none of them raises the question of its *cultivation* as directly as a conversation I had many years ago with the president of a Japanese university.

I am sure you have had the experience of feeling in especially high spirits and good humor when you suddenly run into a stranger in need of help. You go out of your way to lend a hand without giving it a second thought. But when you are in a sour mood, the second thoughts tend to take over. You "mind" the inconvenience and give yourself an excuse to pass by. In both cases you are aware and make a choice. How you are feeling at the moment does not affect the central fact: someone needs help and you are able to give it. As an overall policy, what is the best way to be helpful? Surely you don't want to forfeit the special sensitivity to others that cheerfulness excites in you and the potential effect it can have. At the same time, you cannot count on your feelings to align with those who ask you for assistance. If you allow your feelings to govern your actions, the times when you are out of sorts will have you thinking of yourself instead of the one in need.

Put yourself, now, in the position of the manager of a store who has to instruct his staff how to behave to customers from behind the counter. This was the question the president of a major chain of department stores in Japan asked my friend the university president to address before an auditorium full of employees.

"I told them to think of all the people whose lives they come into contact with every day through helping them make a purchase. They smile as they have been trained to do, never straying from the role of the gracious assistant, never intruding into questions they have not been asked to answer, never allowing their own feelings at the moment to affect their equal and even-tempered treatment of each and every client. *The customer is a god*, as the proverb goes, and as such is to be treated with deference by keeping themselves at a respectful distance.

"But what would happen," he went on, "if you put something *behind* that smile? What if you were to wish them well without saying a word, just thinking it to yourself? You come across people who are obviously sad or upset or just worn out, and you give them the same empty smile as if the only thing that mattered were the transaction that brought them to you. Imagine the good you could do by showing compassion for their gloominess or brightening their happiness just by the look in your eyes! So many people, so many wasted opportunities to do good...."

I remember being impressed by the simple message this celebrated scholar of economics and someone I considered a dear friend had chosen for his audience. When I told him so, he leaned in towards me, his face clouded over and bewildered.

"Do you know what the president of the company said to me later that night at supper, after he had consumed enough sake to loosen his tongue?, 'What you told our workers today, it was interesting, but it is the *exact opposite* of what we tell them.'"

His view was that it is better to have employees freeze their smiles and empty themselves of any personal feelings they may happen to have on any particular day or towards any particular customer. Putting their own predispositions on hold and erasing emotional contact from the transaction is a guarantee that everyone is treated the same. My friend had to concede that the matter was not as simple as he had thought.

I don't recall where our discussion went after that, only that his doubts followed me home. I have related that conversation many times since and even taken a certain delight in seeing others share my disquiet over the dilemma. I am too ignorant of what goes into managing a department store to come down on one side or the other as a general policy, or merely to chalk it up to "cultural" differences. Still, it does drive us to draw the line between politeness and civility more clearly.

Politeness and good manners are habits that we rely on precisely because we do not have to think about them most of the time. Their exercise is their own reward. When we are polite, others tend to be polite back to us. The need for civility arises when those habits malfunction or are not enough. Faced with impoliteness, I have to make a choice that mere habit cannot decide for me. I can keep my feelings to myself and just ignore it. Or I can confront the one responsible, which may or may not do any good, but at least it will assure me that *my* habits are the right ones. In either case, I think generically to avoid having to think any further. In order to think collectively, to take in the whole of the situation, I have first to withdraw from reliance on habitual modes of behavior. Only then can I decide what is the civil thing to say—or not say.

Of course, the better choice all around for salespersons is to brush off impoliteness rather than reproach their ill-mannered clients directly. When things get out of hand, the first reaction is often to call over a manager, which is itself a mild form of reproach that may have a calming effect. Even so, it just lays the affair at someone else's feet and avoids the responsibility of sidestepping the learned, habitual response and trying to find a common, civil ground with the disgruntled customer. So, no, I do not think the dilemma of the two presidents is an accurate description of the choices available to the employees of a department store, any more than I think passing judgment or ignoring judgment are the only options we have when we are caught up in someone else's bad manners. When incivility challenges our habits, there are times we need to stand fast as surely as there are times to release ourselves from their hold over us.

How habits of thinking and acting form and harden, how the role of habitual reaction dominates or recedes depending on the circumstances, how habits change over time on their own or with conscious effort—these are among the great mysteries of human psychology with which all of us have to wrestle. I am not suggesting that civility changes one's own habits or those of others. All of us have learned, usually the hard way, that we don't have to hector people whose ideas or ways we find disagreeable, that there are other ways to disagree. When these lessons become habitual in our behavior and manners, we can rely on them. Habits work best when you don't have to stop and think about them. Civility behind the counter does not supersede the equanimity of keeping a habitual smile on one's face and not inflicting oneself on every situation, but it does ask one to be alert to those moments when something more is needed. Perhaps only once a day, or once a week, or even less. But whenever you respond with conscious civility, you are also conscious of the limits of your habitual response. In a word, civility brings consciousness to habit.

The choice to be civil can enter the story of your lives as a tempest, but more often it is experienced as a mild breeze that only grazes your cheek and yet seems to squeeze your whole soul into the moment and tells you what you are made of and what humanity is made of in a way that no amount of rumination over memories can. The stories that make up your identity are richer for the enthusiasm that comes from having taken part in an act of civility that is not yours to claim as your own. From the time we were children we learned how to safeguard ourselves by telling stories to avoid blame or take credit. And indeed, many of the stories we tell as adults to reconfirm our idea of who we are and advertise it to others are of this sort. But the stories that *save* are those that remove us from center stage. Acts of civility change the way we tell the story of our lives by curing us of the idea that the whole of our humanity is wrapped up in our own skins. Our joys and our sorrows are deeper in the knowledge that others have experienced the same thing. The simplest, most unpresumptuous act of civility can open out onto a landscape in which the habits and memories we rely on when we say "I" feel smaller and yet, strangely, all the greater.

Six

Early one morning I entered the grounds of the Ryōan-ji temple in Kyoto with Cardinal Carlo Martini of Milan. I introduced him to the abbot of the monastery and headed over on my own to the famous rock garden. The grounds were not yet opened for visitors and I found myself alone except for a young monk seated at one end. After a few minutes, the monk walked over and sat down next to me on a bench overlooking the garden. His face was somber as he began to instruct me.

"This place is a great mystery, you know. I come here every morning to meditate and it still puzzles me. It has been baffling people like me for more than five hundred years. Some of them think that it only tricks the onlooker into thinking it has a meaning when it has none. As for me, I want to keep an open mind, which is why I sit here day after day brooding, waiting for the garden to reveal its secret...."

And so he went on and on. I began to feel sorry for the poor fellow, but it would have been cruel to suggest that he might be just wasting his time. Then it struck me. I'm not sure why I said what I said, only that I wanted to lighten his mood.

"Do you know Simon and Garfunkel?"

"Sure, I love their songs."

"So you probably know 'I am a Rock.' Maybe that's your answer."

I was having him on, but rather than just laugh, he took me seriously and stared back expectantly. Either I had to admit I was just teasing or find another way out. I decided to improvise.

"There are fifteen rocks in the garden, right? And wherever you sit on these benches, you can only see fourteen of them. Well, 'I' am the rock you cannot see. Isn't that what you try to understand in Zen meditation, that no matter where you stand in the world, you cannot see the 'I'? You think you see it and then it turns out to be something else. Looking for the hidden rock is the hopeless quest for the 'I.' What seems like a deep mystery is really nothing more than a shadow that clouds the mind."

I will never forget what happened next. He rolled his eyes upwards, stood up, and walked off waving his index finger and mumbling to himself, "*I* am the rock. *I* am the rock...," until he disappeared down the road that led out of the temple.

Oh my! What had I done? I wanted him to stop and take himself less seriously for a moment, not *more*. Had I just pushed a mind running around in circles one way to run in the opposite direction? By the time I ran to catch up with him, he was long gone. I never saw him again.

Like many things we catch ourselves saying without really appreciating their meaning until later, there was more to my words than I knew. We like to think that wisdom emerges from deep reflection, but the truth is, it can come over any of us—unexpectedly and undeserved. What does the psalmist say? "Out of the mouth of babes...." I had wanted to teach the monk a lesson about self-importance, but he had prompted me to say something about the rock garden that might not otherwise have occurred to me.

The episode at Ryōan-ji pushes our discussion of civility beyond interpersonal relationships. No matter where you stand to look at the natural world, human beings are never at the center. Nature is not an "environment" for humans. Our history on this planet is too short for such hubris. In fact, it is not an environment at all, because there is no center around which everything else revolves. Or perhaps better put, its center is everywhere. Each element or cluster of elements is a point at which the whole world is concentrated just this once and never again. Any privileged position we give to human life is our own doing. The world was in the making long before we evolved onto the scene. It remains a miracle of connections that far exceeds anything we might accomplish in the attempt to claim it as *our* environment. Our praise of civility would be incomplete if it excluded the earth.

Genius is no excuse for incivility. (Richard Wagner is a case in point. The poet W. H. Auden is reported to have called him "indisputably a genius, but apart from that an absolute shit.") So, too, the advance of civilization is no excuse for incivility in our administration of the natural world. When we refer to the rest of the planet as "non-human" in order to excuse our ravage of its resources, we are employing the worst sort of argument: *ad hominem*, which roughly translates to "argument by insult." Logically, no debate is "won" by having one party browbeaten into standing down. The aim of such a story is to dismiss the dispute, not see it through.

Nothing is more noxious to civility than using insult as a weapon. To make oneself the cornerstone of an interaction dooms the construction to collapse; to bicker in self-serving clichés nails a living discussion in its coffin. When an exchange of ideas becomes an altercation and arguments become argumentative, the goal is no longer to find out which side is correct, or if correctness lies somewhere in between the competing views, but to win, and to inflate one's image in the process. When I think of all the corrections and reproofs I have meted out to others or suffered at their hands from my boyhood days up to the present, I have to say they had their most lasting impact when they were spoken without malice or contempt. Nastiness can be effective, but always at a cost. When someone leaves your presence thinking less of themselves than when they entered, you are deflated as much as they. Incivility is a self-inflicted wound.

Much the same can be said of the *ad naturam* logic of molesting the earth and silencing its voice. From the time we learned to control fire and began to forge tools, humankind have been caught up in an argument with the forces of nature. Civilization has progressed not only by using nature's laws to it own advantage, but also by taking the law into its own hands. As we grow more conscious of how the rewards of winning have locked nature out of the conversation, so, too, have we come to question the logic of insult at work in the background. The inflation of our self-image as masters of everything below us on the evolutionary hierarchy has arrived at a threshold that threatens civilization itself.

The meek, it is said, will inherit the earth. Surely it will not be by cowering to the insolence of those who disparage the rights of the non-human. To inherit the earth, in all its history and diversity, in its strengths and fragilities, requires the same mind that enables us to inherit the history, diversity, strengths, and fragilities of our own human nature: a mind that thinks selflessly, collectively, convivially. This, and not a mere flat-earth docility, is what it means to be meek.

Sharpening our sense of conviviality with the planet has reinvigorated the imagery that anthropomorphizes our alliances to the natural world, using relationships between people as a metaphor for the way we relate to nature. The problem is that the measure of the relationship remains tied to our definition of human being. To keep a balance, we also need to look at things from the other side of the fence, where we are not in control of the imagery. From that perspective, the response of the forces of nature to our excesses in transforming the earth into the best possible environment for human civilization may be seen as a metaphor for the practice of civility in human society.

When we spoke earlier of acting *naturally* by removing the heroic ego from the center of a situation, we meant following the deeper impulses of our humanity. But this does not eclipse the fact that the whole of our nature is wrapped in a greater nature, whose native impulses feed into everything we claim to be distinctively human. When I follow the dictates of my heart or my conscience, I am not acting supernaturally vis-à-vis the laws that govern the rest of the natural world. I embody those laws, no less than the apple falling downwards to the ground or the owl preying on a rabbit. The difference is the level of control that consciousness brings—that special wonder of wonders in evolution that we call "freedom." Deep-rooted as the idea is in our philosophies and psychologies and legal systems, this freedom of ours is haunted by the paradox that we are not free to understand what it actually means. This is never clearer to us than when our impulses straddle the borderline between human nature and nature writ large, one foot planted in the urge to decide, the other planted in the urge to let go. It is here that we replace talk of freedom with equally perplexing notions like "fate" or "destiny," where the anthropomorphic lining of our place in the order of things is turned inside out.

I am reminded of a discussion about ethics with a small circle of colleagues and friends in Kyoto. Actually, the only part I remember is a story that Zen master Hirata Seikō of Tenryū-ji temple recounted about one of his predecessors. It was after the War and people were lost. Disillusioned at their political and religious leaders, they felt like small animals at bay before the monster of despair. Anxieties about how to feed their families and get the medical attention they needed, how to trust the education of their children to a system that had betrayed them and how to restore their pride as a nation, huddled together in the paralyzing reality of defeat. A public talk by a local monk was announced with the title, "What are we to do now?" The monk stepped onto the stage to face the sea of faces that had gathered to listen. Silence fell over the hall.

"Imagine that you are standing at bank of a river on a winter's day, watching the swift, freezing waters flow by. You see two figures standing in the middle of a nearby bridge upriver, your mother and your wife pregnant with your first child. Suddenly the bridge collapses and both of them are thrown into the icy stream. Realizing that you can only save one of them, which one do you save?"

With that, the monk dropped the microphone to his side and looked out expectantly. After a minute, someone in the audience stood up.

"I would save my mother. Our relationship goes back to the beginning and I should honor it above all others."

And so the debate began.

"Yes," another voice spoke up, "but when you start a new family, they take first place. I would save my wife."

"And besides, when you save the wife, you save two people."

"But your mother, no one can ever replace her..."

After some time, a woman from the back of the hall interrupted and addressed the monk on stage.

"But this is supposed to be *your* talk. Which one would *you* save?"

The venerable old man smiled. "Whichever one is closest to me."

There are times when momentous, even life-changing, choices are forced on us that we lack the time or resources to reason about. The confusion that nature spins in the brains of its children when they have come to their limits is not the cosmos sneering at our petty pretense to freedom. It is part of the birthright to freedom.

No one in the hall could have failed to understand that much from the monk's reply. Even when we lack the means to reason our way to a free choice, when circumstances overwhelm our sense of what is good and right but still press us to act, the freedom to decide what to do next is no longer something I own. It is something that owns me. Without an innate sense of our connectedness to the natural world, we would be immobilized.

Responding to whatever need is closest is our way of leaning on nature when our own legs no longer support us. Understanding with Heraclitus that "everything flows" does not bring moral clarity or generate moral injunctions. At most, it prompts us to resign ourselves to the things we are not free to change. The confluence and transitoriness of all things that swept the two women past the outstretched arm of their son and husband belong to a rhythm that transcends our own. Civility towards the earth begins with that insight.

Our ongoing "argument" with the earth over control of its laws is a struggle as complex and prone to conflict as the overlapping of human nature and nature writ large, of freedom and destiny, of reason and the reality that overflows its bounds. There once was a natural world without humans and one day there will be again. For all we know, such worlds exist elsewhere in the vast expanse of the cosmos. Meantime, so long as we reject that idea of a dualism between the human and natural realms, and accept that everything is inextricably connected with everything else, civility will have its part to play in that argument.

To say everything is connected and that the stories of reason are all wrapped in a greater story does not mean that reality itself is a kind of central nervous system managed by a single brain, like a great Puppet Master positioned above all the connections to keep the strings from getting tangled. It means only that fate—that which must naturally come to pass—shadows our freedom to think and decide without eclipsing it. At those times when we find ourselves driven to the borderline of our ability to administer the laws of nature and look into the faceless abyss, we face the ultimate choice we can make as human beings, to cry out in despair or to murmur the words of an ancient Aztec prayer to the heavens, "We thank you for loaning us for a short while to each other."

It is only when we turn back to face the demands of connectedness in everyday life that the choice not to despair of our human condition can affect our relationships with one another and with the earth. As obvious as that sounds, the failures and desperations can pile up and eat away at our fundamental gratitude for being alive. So much of what we work so hard to build up falls apart in the end, through no fault of our own. The more the process is repeated, the greater the temptation to lose trust in our freedom and resign ourselves to the powers that be. The more I try to be civil, it seems, the less impact I have on events. Time and again the "real world" takes me by the scruff of the neck and shakes me into compliance. Respect for other people and for the rights of the natural world is met with the scorn of individuals and structures coded to protect themselves against reform. My original idealism transforms itself into a competing ideology or simply concedes defeat by turning its coat with the tides of opinion, withering into cynicism, or hitching its credulity to the nearest castle in cloud cuckoo land.

That on the one hand. On the other, legends of individuals who held fast to their ideals against all odds can be found in the inspirational antiquaries of all times and places. The most heroic of them are those not driven by an heroic ego set on the accomplishment of noble deeds, but by the forgoing of reward in the name of something greater than themselves. Consider the story of the seventeenth-century Zen monk Tetsugen Dōkō, which to this day lives in the imagination of Japanese children as an example of heroism in failure.

As a young man of twenty-five, Tetsugen left the Pure Land tradition into which he had been ordained and entered a Zen monastery, abandoning his wife and family. Beset by doubts over his chosen path, he eventually found his footing. He began to teach and take on disciples, all the while rising in the ranks of the establishment. It was when he turned to a grander undertaking that his personal struggles and ambitions loosened their control over his life. At the time, copies of the sacred scriptures in use by the various Buddhist schools across the country were scarce and the Chinese versions they were based on were often riddled with errors. Tetsugen's dream was to compile a new Japanese edition of the Buddhist canon and make it readily available.

For that, he would need a temple to house the texts he had received from China and the new woodblocks, a print shop, trained woodcarvers, and an office for sales and distribution—all of which took money, a lot of it. Begging for alms in the streets was not enough. He organized a broad campaign aimed at wealthy donors and worked tirelessly at the task for thirteen years until at last he had secured the necessary funds to begin. After twelve years and 60,000 woodblocks later, the first editions were ready for print, two years before Tetsugen's death at age fifty-two.

The completion of the project secured Tetsugen a place of honor in the history of Buddhism, but it was the actions he took to impede its completion that made him a lasting symbol of human greatness. As the legend goes, while Tetsugen was in the midst of raising funds, the Uji River south of Kyoto overflowed its banks, carrying away many to their deaths and bringing famine to many others. Tetsugen took the money he had collected and donated it to save others from starvation. Undeterred, he began to gather funds again.

Several years later, an epidemic broke out and spread quickly through the populace. Once more, he gave away what he had collected to aid the sick and dying. He returned to his project for a third time and was able at last to see it through to the end. As the children are told, Tetsugen made three sets of sutras, only the last of which found its way into print. The first two were invisible, but had a greater impact. It is a truth as old as our philosophies and religions: teachings engraved into blocks of wood and inked on paper are never as valuable or as real as teachings woven into the stuff of people's lives.

You may think we have strayed far from the praise of civility, but we have actually wound our way back to where we began. True civility is not heroic in the ordinary sense of the term. It is not memorialized in monuments. It is not decorated or compensated with rewards. It is not registered in our annals or coded into our laws or customs. It is not taught through discipline or rational argument. Its attachment to particular individuals or particular events is fleeting; its evidence, circumstantial. That is precisely what makes it all the more durable and worthy of all the praise we can accord it.

The occasions where civility is called for are few. For the most part, we glide through our daily interactions trusting in the norms of good behavior and proper etiquette. When differences of opinion arise, or when we are affronted by thoughtless behavior or ill-intentioned remarks, we all have our ways to glide over them without breaking pace. When they touch too close to home and threaten harm, we may choose to stop in our tracks and take a stance.

But sometimes, just sometimes, the better choice is to step back from yourself, refrain from judgment, gather in as much as you can of the situation, and do the civil thing. We *know* when those times are, but the prospect of losing control to stupidity or malevolence makes the better choice the less appealing one. We know from watching others, or at least we think we know, the surest way to walk away a winner. And this is a large part of the problem.

Chief Sitting Bull of the Lakota Nation was nicknamed "Slow" for his pensive and unhurried manner. Despite the violent rush of history in which he played a leading role, he is also revered for his teachings on generosity to others. "Inside of me," he said, "there are two dogs. One of them is mean and evil, the other is good. They fight with each constantly. When asked which one wins, my answer is: whichever I feed the most."

It is we who do the feeding, but the fodder is provided by what we see going on around us. As Sitting Bull would learn at the battle of Little Big Horn, it would be foolhardy to think that the good dog is always the self-effacing and docile dog, or that resistance and indignation are always signs that the self-righteous and violent dog has taken over. Civility, we have been insisting, has its place, but it can also be out of place. When civility is in place, things are not about you; subtraction of judgment is more important than addition.

It is no less foolhardy to trust that you always know, on your own, when it is the proper response and when not. To say that the impulse to civility and the knowledge of when it is called for is "natural" does not mean that it is baked into our nature as the skin-bound individuals we are. Consciousness of our truest and most trustworthy impulses does not emerge full grown like Venus arising out of the sea. It grows and takes shape through imitation of what we learn from the complex, erratic, and unpredictable web of connections that makes us social beings. Everything I say that "I know" is always something "I know *we* know." The choices I make are not only my own; they are also social constructions. The choice to take a step back from generic or conventional thinking in order respond with civility is a reconnection with something I know we know about human nature. It is natural not because I believe it to be mine, but because I trust it to be ours.

It is easy to think of the distinction between social

knowledge and personal knowledge as a teeter-totter that lifts me up to my own identity and then drops me back down into a community of other individuals eager to maintain theirs. The reality is not so simple. The skills I use to keep the seesaw moving were learned in the very community from which I wish to distinguish myself and against which I wish to defend my freedoms. Imitation is a large part of the way I go about defining who I am, deciding which dog I choose to feed and what I choose to feed it. Legends of saints and sages passed on from one generation to the next set the background for imitation and provide perspective, but the broad strokes in which their stories are told overlap too unevenly with our own lives to be imitated directly.

The figures we set in the foreground make all the difference here. My admiration for Tetsugen's perseverance and self-detachment only comes alive if it turns my attention to examples closer to home, like the poor couple across town who have to sacrifice everything to keep their children fed and clothed. Precisely because their story is not the stuff of legend, their everyday struggles chafe at my own conceit and press on me to emulate their courage.

I once chaired a lecture by Gustavo Gutiérrez, a Peruvian priest who had gained attention around the world for his efforts to alert Christian doctrine to its subtle but powerful bonds to institutionalized poverty and injustice. Like others who accompanied him in the cause of "liberation theology," he had incited the ire of the establishment around Latin America and eventually of the authorities in Rome.

The discussion had gone on for nearly three hours and I was about to wrap things up so that people could go home for supper, when one of the audience waved his hand furiously. I decided to take one last question. It was about the condemnation leveled against Dr. Gutiérrez's writings by the Roman Curia for their Marxist leanings.

His modest and unassuming reply did not hide the suffering his summons to Rome had caused him and the unfairness with which he had been treated as a loyal member of the church dedicated to the forgotten poor. Some in the assembly were visibly upset by the revelation, but one could see the change in their expression as he went on.

"In a few days, I will be back in the small church where I celebrate Mass on Sunday. And there, in the front row, will be Maria with her three small children. She will come in the same tattered dress she wears every week. Her children will be in the Sunday best that she can afford only by sacrificing everything to make the best possible life for them. When I think of what I suffered for my writings in comparison with what Maria goes through every day for her children..., *no es nada—absolutamente nada.*"

His words thundered through the hall. There was no need to translate them. After a few moments of silence that seemed to sweep us up into the sheer humanity of what we had just heard, the audience stood up to applaud.

Every soul of us gathered there learned something important that day. I have no doubt I was not alone in wishing I had the courage to measure my life on the same scale.

So, too, the only way to offset the examples of incivility we see all about us is to see through them and learn to trust in the ordinary, undramatic examples of civility that we would see if only we took the time to look more closely. We are always imitating, but we do not need to be swept away by the prevailing tides. How often in our discussions do we not mimic the way opinion leaders deal with one another as a reason for engaging in their incivility, and admire the pundits who uphold our side. All too commonly, the intensity of public debate is fueled by generalizations and principles, drawing the lines between pro and con in a way that makes it difficult for them and their listeners to take a position that honors difference of opinion. This is not a model for our daily interactions. The more it governs our day and night, the more it becomes self-destructive—and a nightmare for anyone who lives with us or counts on us for their trust in our better instincts.

Our praise of civility would be wasted if the result were to turn attention away from imitation and merely inflate the armory of reasons for condemning incivility in others as a roadblock to our preoccupations with "bigger" issues. As virtues and vices go, civility and incivility may seem to huddle at the low end of the spectrum together with petty goodness and petty evil, the very place from which we smile at the simplicity of children who cannot handle the complicated problems of life.

Nevertheless, at those times when we are obliged to look at our lives against the broader landscape of what is best in our humanity, we cannot help thinking of what we have lost from our childhood in the process of growing up: the sense of wonder before the simplest yet most powerful ideas we have. Our minds, muddled by the tidal wave of opinion and counter-opinion have abandoned ideas like love and peace and justice into a fog almost too thick to penetrate.

How badly we wish at times that others would look at us as if for the first time, the way children do. Yet, how rarely we see ourselves or others that way. Civility is nothing if not the childlike sense of wonder that takes you a step back—into the naive simplicity of your ideals and out of the pessimism of the fog.

The potential we have as children has always to contend with what others make of us, some of which feeds our mean and evil dog. There is no way to become what you are without stepping out of the fog and deciding for yourself what you want to guide you. Without that, imitation risks collapsing into mimicry. Instead of tending to the seeds asleep within us from our youth, we rely on fruit from the orchards of our matured selves. We know what it is for the emotional earthquake of personal loss or tragedy to shake us out of that reliance and awaken us to those neglected ideals and dreams that we were never quite able to leave behind completely. I am convinced that the feeling of being swept up in the simplest act of civility can do the same—so long as you let its echoes bounce off your everyday modes of thought and behavior.

Is there something in you that cannot seem to find its voice? Think of the last time you had something to communicate but could not come up with the words for it.

Is there something in you that does not feel "at home"? Think of the last time you were in comfortable surroundings and suddenly became aware of being out of place.

Is there something in you that does not fit in the world? The cultural encoding that governs your life is by and large as transparent as the air, but there are always those times when you feel an outsider and find it hard to breathe.

Is there something in you that you are convinced no one gave you? Not your parents, your grandparents, not anyone—something outside of the gene pool and outside of your upbringing.

Have you ever felt a darkness in you that you cannot see—some mysterious corner of yourself that you try to think about and look at, but which is always just out of sight?

Is there some weak point in your personality that embarrasses you before others and yet makes you feel your strongest—someplace where you can let go and feel as if you have the whole world in your hands?

What you sense when you answer these questions is a wellspring that can be released into your life if you can just find it in yourself to get out of the way. Civility, I am persuaded, is one way to do just that.

Seven

The first-century Greek philosopher Epictetus, born a slave and freed at the age of eighteen, devoted his teachings to liberating people from what he called "the slavery of the soul." Ever since I was a young graduate student, his *Discourses* has been part of that short shelf of books I open at random to clear my head. For all his insistence on the practice of one's convictions, Epictetus' head-in-the-clouds idealism is just the thing when the feet-on-the-ground slog through daily life becomes too much to bear. Two of his remarks about thieves come to mind here.

"We get angry because we put too high a premium on things that they can steal. Don't attach such value to your clothes, and you won't get angry with the thief who takes them." (In fairness to the text, the passage continues with a statement we find it hard to excuse, despite its antiquity: "Don't make your wife's external beauty her chief attraction, and you won't be angry with the adulterer.")

The second remark is a reflection on what happened after a thief made off with an iron lamp he kept by his household shrine: "This is how I came to lose my lamp: the thief was more vigilant than I. But he acquired the lamp at a price: he became a thief for its sake and forfeited his honesty; for a lamp, he became a brute. And he imagined he came out ahead!"

Self-awareness and detachment are the core of Epictetus' image of the free mind, namely, the ability to *see clearly what there is to see*. The thief who cannot see what he gave up in exchange for his cleverness, and the householder who clings too tightly to his possessions to recognize their true value, are equally misguided. Their identity is enslaved in the very things we have been pointing to as the principal disincentives to civility.

To dismiss Epictetus' words as only meaningful to those who already agree with him takes us nowhere. Granted, ethics by aphorism is a lame ersatz for conscience. Yet, time spent in the sensation of freedom that comes with stories of detached and wide-eyed civility—both our own and those of others—is not an idle luxury. It is an exercise of the one of our greatest treasures: the power to imagine what it would be like to be possessed of that same freedom ourselves.

The rest of the world, as we noted earlier, forgets nothing; it just cannot replay what it has recorded. If you have read Gabriel Garcia-Márquez's magical novel *One Hundred Years of Solitude*, you will recall the epidemic of amnesia that overtook the small village of Macondo. The villagers began to forget the names of things and had to hang signs on them so they would know what they were and what they were for. In context, the image was about the effects of the colonization of one culture by another, but it also speaks to our point here. We do not know what civility is or remember what it is for if all we have to rely on are the sayings of old philosophers or a memo hung on a bunch of examples. It is only a living ideal if we are aware of it in thought and action.

Like it or not, you have to admit that your incivilities have, at times, brought you a certain satisfaction, sweet vengeance, even joy, that has a way of remaining fresh in your mind. But like a grudge borne against another, these memories punish you more than they do the object of your conquest. They are a weight you carry around with you, eroding the very ideals you deceive yourself into thinking you are standing up for. In the end, repressing these memories or driving them out of view with other memories, is self-defeating. The only ideals that can be effective are those that include the memory of our failures to practice them.

In the Greek myth of the afterlife, those who enter the Elysian fields of paradise forget the sins and failings of the past. Only the pleasantest of recollections last for all eternity. This purging of memory is the work of the River of Forgetfulness that leads into that impossible paradise without ideals and meant only for those who choose to forget the past that made them who they are. As long as we fumble our way around this side of the River in search of a good life, our experiments with humanity cannot afford to dispatch with our failures so swiftly.

Among Paul Valéry's *Histoires brisées* is a brief account of the punishment meted out to a certain Xios. "I command you to die," said the King, "but as Xios and not as you." His name and past were changed. When he tried to insist on who he really was, people refuted him with the records. Is this not the very punishment we inflict on ourselves each time we disfigure memory into an Elysian fields of our own concoction?

Of course, we all prefer to hide our crimes and punishments from others. There is the past we present in public and the past we try to keep private, fearing the judgment of others. It is *how* we keep them private that makes all the difference. If the only goal is to immunize ourselves against discovery, we misrelate the facts or garble questions to better fit the answers we have already decided on. But if the goal is to continue experimenting, we need the kind of self-awareness and detachment that Epictetus was talking about. Think back a couple of pages to how you first reacted to his recriminations against the thief and the householder and you will see what I mean.

Getting over your past without forgetting it means breaking your attachment to the meaning you give it. You make a snap judgment on the spur of the moment and a few minutes later have to take it back. This is not forgetting; it's remembering better. There is an Arabic story of two friends walking across the desert. They began to discuss and one of them felt buffeted and shamed because his companion was more learned and intelligent. Unable to discuss any further, he bent down and wrote in the sand. "Today my best friend slapped at me."

After a while they came upon an oasis and stopped to refresh themselves. As the one who had been shamed put his foot into the waters, he slipped on the mud and fell into the pool. His friend reached out and saved him from drowning. He took a chisel from his pack and inscribed these words on a nearby rock: "Today my best friend saved my life."

When they were back on their way, his friend asked him why he wrote first in the sand and later in stone.

"When someone offends you, leave it to the winds of oblivion and pardon to erase. But when they help you, write it in your heart where no wind on earth can ever touch it."

The wind erased the words, but not the insult, which merely altered its place in the memory of the past. When we retell the story of our lives, judgments that were front and center in our emotions often slip to the periphery, and vice versa. To resist changing the story is to freeze memory in place.

Detachment from certitudes is always uncomfortable. It can signal a sea change in one's identity, which can occur slowly over time, through the tempered accumulation of doubts, or abruptly through a sharp and unexpected awakening. The easiest response is to replace one certitude with another, leaving the attachment intact.

It is said that Diogenes was eating bread and beans for supper when he was approached by the philosopher Aristippus, who had secured comfortable living for himself by flattering the whims of the king.

"If you would learn to be servile to the king you would not have to live on bread and beans."

"Learn to live on bread and beans," replied Diogenes, "and you will not have to be subservient to the king."

Servility to a king is not something we have to worry about in modern-day democracies. But deposing a monarchy does not, by itself, immunize us against servility. In the absence of a monarch, the desire for security through allegiance to something beyond question does not diminish. The empty throne cries out for certitudes to assume sovereignty over our lives. Flattering the whims of our certitudes has its advantages, but at a price.

I don't mean to suggest that you clutter your mind with more uncertainties. Life has a way of supplying us with more than we can handle as it is. That said, when civility is allowed to run its course, it is bound at times to discompose the sturdiest habits of thought and expose their untruth. Admittedly, the mind is paralyzed without assumptions; but this does not mean those assumptions have to be hidden in certitudes. On the contrary, the ability to convert certitudes into working assumptions is the only way the mind has to escape the temptation to servility and obsession. So long as we are conscious of the fact that our assumptions are at work, we can accept or reject or transform them. To take them out of their working conditions and imagine them as beyond history and culture and societal change is to let them take custody of our natural impulses and rule over us like the king and his groveling minion Aristippus.

The mere mention of "certitude" inevitably steers us in the troublesome waters of religious faith. At the risk of offending, and knowing full well that my conclusions leak at every joint, the lure is too great to resist.

When I look over the religions whose texts I hold in special esteem and whose rituals have brought me solace at difficult times in life, I do not see them primarily as institutions, as funds of doctrine, as sets of moral principles, or even as paths to personal salvation, but as ways of reconnecting with the things of life, with the people in my life, and with the natural world.

In religion, as in any body of principles, certitude frosts the glass of received wisdom, blocking its truth from sight by sanctifying the patterns on the surface. Whenever I see established organizations, doctrines, moral precepts, beliefs in another world, and the search for peace of mind impede that reconnection, my every instinct tells me to shake the dust off my sandals and turn away. Whenever religious teachings are expropriated for the therapeutic engineering of thought and conduct, they desert their origins and our ability to discover those origins in the impulses of our own nature. Like any bridge built of certitudes, blind attachment to religion easily leads to institutional or ideological servitude in one form or another.

Varieties of religious tradition and all their social utility aside, the essence of faith is the intersection of a sense of *time*—which is visible to us in the pace of daily life and the records of our collective history—and a sense of *eternity*—which is invisible, unknowable, uncontrollable. How you choose to imagine the architecture of eternity or to name its power is secondary to the ability to detect its intersection with the time of your own life as more than a snag in your routine. To awaken that ability and impel it to practical consequences, religion must finally dispel the illusion that its own teachings and practices constitute the essence of faith. The communication of faith relies mightily on religious symbols and stories, but until it can see through them to the possibility of rhythms that transcend our own, it is only halfway to its destination.

The Japanese style of pottery known as *kintsuki* is a good image of faith without certitude. It dates back to a fifteenth century art of creating beauty through the repair of broken teacups. A lacquer mixed with gold dust is used to fix the pieces back together. The veins of gold show both the wounds and their healing in a way that a smooth glaze cannot. They give value to the finished composition at the same time as they highlight the fragility of its origins. What you hold in your hands is the restoration of a broken past, an image of the temporary nature of all our handiwork intersecting with the desire to overcome it. It reconnects time, which moves from one fragmentation to the next, to the irrepressible but always uncertain longing for reparation. The germ of religious faith lies asleep in the soil of that longing, waiting only to be awakened from its slumber.

At its very best, religion, like art, does something to language that excites us and frightens us at the same time. It detaches us from everyday certitudes without disconnecting us from the transiency of the everyday.

Across the plaza from the apartment in Barcelona where I often stay when I am in the city, stands the Basilica of Santa María del Mar. To step in, as I often do, is to be embraced at once by the grandeur of its space, to feel one's eyes and spirit elevated beyond the concerns of the day. I forget where I have come from and where I am going. If only for a brief moment, I am transported to a place higher than myself. The narrow horizons of my day open up; it is as if I were looking down at myself from the top of the dome. You must know the feeling. It is not an illusion of architecture but a longing from within for something beyond description that we need to survive.

On leaving, I often have to step over beggars holding up signs about their illness or being out of work and having a household of children to feed. Like many residents in the area, I tend to be skeptical of their solicitations. There are too many professional beggars around to know which of them is truly deserving of help. But then again, there are all those stories about down-and-outs paying doctors to cut off a hand or a foot to better their chances of collecting alms. I am appalled at the thought and wonder what could drive people to mutilate themselves in this way. At the same time, I am annoyed to find myself overcome by a sense of pity, which only fortifies the wall between me and the less fortunate. Depending on which of these tangled emotions gets the better of me, I either reach in my pocket or pretend not to notice.

And yet, there are times when I react before my assumptions get involved, before my thoughts can line themselves up logically, and without any sense of generosity or compassion empty my coin purse in the nearest outstretched hand. The spontaneous and uncredited gesture is not something I can say I decided to do. It was something I participated in, from that place higher than myself that followed me out onto the steps of the basilica. I am sure you recognize this feeling, too, as one of those moments when you reconnect with eternity in time, a moment of sheer faith and civility for which you can never quite find the words.

Civility belongs to the present, fully and without judgment. It has no master plan to rehabilitate a life too fragmented for any vein of gold to fashion into a single story with a beginning and an end. Its fullness is the way it touches the whole of one's being, in the blink of an eye, and then withdraws the touch. No narrative that claims to bring harmony to the whole muddle of existence is any match for the overwhelming ambiguity that comes from having a mind that can ask questions too big for it to answer. To entrust permanent custody of our ideals to fixed ideas of right and wrong, true and false, is to put the fullness of time—those moments when time and eternity intersect—out of reach.

You do not understand the beauty of the nightingale's song by transcribing it into a score. You do not understand the creative power of reason unless you know how to give reason a rest. The creation story of the Achomawi of northeast California tells us that in the beginning there was only a coyote and a silver fox. The fox told the coyote to take a nap and, when he had fallen asleep, combed out his hair and laid it out over the water, creating land. Creativity needs sleep. In the biblical story, too, Yahweh's first gift to Adam was not Eve but the sleep from which she was created. Giving reason a rest is not being unreasonable. It is suspending reason in order to release it from the congestion of overwork and free it to see more clearly. Nothing we have to say in praise of civility, none of the examples we have given to show civility in action, is meant to belittle the faculty of reason. On the contrary, it is only by understanding what rational thinking cannot do that we are able to appreciate what it can.

Once we make the assumption that civility is not a struggle *against* human nature but *towards* it, we have every reason to anticipate that, as long as we don't get in the way, some part of it will spill over into situations with which civility alone is woefully unequipped to deal. Civility is not an antidote to everything that poisons human relations, but it is a baseline for beginning to do something about it. Even if you are out on the streets demonstrating or engaged in formal debate against truly dangerous ideas, your assumptions about civility can affect the resolution of your actions. No doubt, good manners and a sense of propriety help keep a lid on emotions boiling aggressively under the surface. Acting with civility is the attempt to do something about them.

The struggle toward what is best in human nature is kinder to truth than attachment to certitudes is, precisely because it is aware that what we call "the truth" is more than acquiescence to objective facts. It always belongs to someone, at some time and in some circumstances, but never to everyone always and everywhere or in the same intensity. The habit of being civil towards those convinced of a truth that is not my own does not change the logic of their reasoning or yours. Nevertheless, as even a moment's reflection on recent disagreements brought to peaceful resolve will remind you, it can loosen the hold that your perception of the facts has over your logical conclusions.

By now it must have occurred to you that my theoretical tirade against certitudes as an impediment to clear thinking, to the convivial pursuit of truth, and to the cultivation of habits of civility does not apply to the lived convictions of religious men and women as easily as it does to more abstract ideas about the essence of faith. Surely those who follow a religious tradition and trust in the truth of its teachings to assure their salvation will bristle at the vulgar charge of "attachment to certitudes." The insolence those words imply is undeserved and does not reflect what they believe or how they exercise those beliefs in their lives.

The point of the rebuff is well taken and forces our critique of certitude to greater caution, as any generalization about religion is bound to. Without going very deeply into the issue, I would note, to begin with, that the deformities of mind deriving from religious certitude are an unlikely measure of the whole of a tradition. Moreover, but less obviously, even the most steadfast commitment to teachings and moral principles believed to have seeped into this world from a reality beyond our own is not primarily an intellectual pledge of allegiance to an abstract fund of truths. It is rather a standpoint for practical insight into the things that matter most in life. If questions about one's attachment to certitudes come to mind at all, what incentive short of an already advanced crisis of faith would there be to match wits with it? So long as religious convictions produce fruit, epistemological speculation is the least of its worries.

I agree. Ultimately, vigilance against the allures of certitude is less important than living out one's most deeply felt convictions. But it is also important for more than philosophical clarity. Convictions move in two directions, the one soaring high into the realm of ideals, the other walking on the ground through the hubbub of practical conduct. Convictions without ideals are disoriented; ideals without practical consequences are empty. Much as we may admire the lives of saints and heroes who seem to move between the two effortlessly, our failure without end to imitate them remove them from the realm of possibility. Perhaps that is why we take greater comfort in those who continue their voyage after their ideals have run aground.

After the death of Mother Teresa of Calcutta in 1997, voices clamoring for her promotion to sainthood echoed around the world. But that final honor was stalled when letters came to light revealing the deep doubt that seemed to cover her faith in an impenetrable darkness. We had known her as a candle that allowed itself to be consumed in order to lighten the lives of those around her, but it was when we saw the flame sputter and the wick struggle to hold on to its dying sparks against the wind that we were able to take heart in the coincidence of her humanity with our own. Regardless of the spiritual insecurity with the ideals that drove her, she carried on until she emerged stronger than before. Beatified in 2003, it was not until 2016 that she was canonized—not in spite of her incertitude but because of it.

Allowing oneself to be ruled by moral indignation chips away at the cast of mind that makes it possible to revere a life like hers and imitate it in ordinary acts of civility. As powerless as she was to effect change in the larger social institutions that closed an eye to the sufferings of those she attended at their dying breath, Mother Teresa showed us something in our humanity that we ignore at our peril. Her image is a lasting embarrassment to the masks of indecency we turn towards those who do not share our certitudes, to the charade of a goodness and virtue that sets itself up as the arbiter of righteousness. Let those charades speak in the language of religion or ethics or politics; let them promote causes liberal or traditionalist, patriotic or cosmopolitan, capitalist or socialist. Nothing they have to say can silence the humble courage of that gaunt slip of a woman from Albania.

The labels of heroism and sanctity, even when hung on the deserving, inevitably make us feel uneasy about ourselves and the tedium of our routine lives by comparison. They falsely suggest that goodness demands fearless, teeth-gritting resolve, when usually it asks for no more than a smile of recognition or a step back from conflict. To those who are unhappy with doing what is right until they can be *seen* to be doing what it is they are doing, unacknowledged goodness is a sign of mediocrity. The civility which I have been trying to hold up to the light does not depend on recognition. Nor is it an extravagance we can allow ourselves at some times but not at others. It is a necessity bred in the instinct to savor as much of our humanity as we can.

As I am sure you realize, I have fixed on the word *civility* as a lodestar to chart a path through personal memories of episodes and images that have battened my enthusiasm for the more congenial tendencies of our nature. Other concepts might have done as well, but *civility* has a kind of seductive, nonsectarian appeal that favors engagement over clarity of definition.

The idea that I might find the place where the young mother in the spiked hair and ripped jeans was standing when she took a step back from the public insult and bowed, where Francis of Assisi was kneeling when he looked into the eyes of the hungry wolf of Gubbio, where Hakuin stood when he shouldered the slander of the villagers patiently until they came to their senses, where the Cretan farmer with his donkey cart was sitting when he told a poor student to save his gratitude for the day he would find himself in the same situation as he, where Tetsugen was grounded when he handed over the funds he had been collecting for years to feed the starving—the idea that I might find that place to say what they said and do what they do pulls at those tendencies in our nature that give us hope against the cynicisms of the age.

How to reread this book

It is not enough to sit in an armchair and read about civility. To borrow an image from Chuan-tse, rushing into the shade of an oak tree will not help you run away from your own shadow. The darkness that your own incivilities cast on your life and the lives of those around you deserve more than a greater darkness. The contribution your own civility can make to the world is something far greater than a book-full of words about it. Nevertheless, if you still feel as I do, that there is much more to be said on the matter, take counsel of your own doubts and read this book again with the fresh eye of hindsight.

Heaven forbid that you should plow through these meanderings of mine again and rummage between the lines in search of something you may have missed. No fruit you might harvest by transplanting the saplings from this greenhouse of ideas into your own reflections will ever ripen as full and sweet as what you can reap by picking out the seeds and scattering them in your own memory and imagination. No, the right way to reread this book is to skip from paragraph to paragraph, gliding past all the analysis and commentary until you come to one of the anecdotes. Read it to yourself, as if for the first time. Then put the book aside and compose your own thoughts on it, guided by whatever feelings it may arouse and drawing on memories of your own that clamor for a voice in the discussion. It makes no matter if your thoughts are random and disconnected. Most of my own were a mishmash of intuitions and unripened insights. Why pot those dry flowers when you can sit among the lilies of the field!

In the end, there is no greater praise you can add to civility than the practical effects it has on your moral bearings, and no fainter praise than a simple reflex of my own admiration of it. Spending time alone, naked and unashamed, in the raw and unblemished sobriety of *knowing* what civility is and consenting to its place in your life, is to imagine your contribution to the world differently. It was in that spirit, so trustworthy and so forceful, that I began, and in that spirit that I come now to an end.

www.ingramcontent.com/pod-product-compliance
Lightning Source LLC
Chambersburg PA
CBHW070455090426
42735CB00012B/2559